To the Best L
gal in the World

I didn't know you
spoke "chenese"!

Ta

Your Loving Dad

Kirkfm

ISBN 0-941676-31-5

CHINESE CUISINE

Szechwan Style

編　　　著	林麗華
出　版　者	純青出版社有限公司
	台北市松江路125號4樓
	郵政劃撥：12106299
	電話：(02) 2508-4331 ・2507-4902
著作財產權人	財團法人味全文化教育基金會
總　經　銷	味全出版社有限公司
	台北市仁愛路4段28號2樓
版　權　所　有	局版台業字第3884號
	中華民國89年9月六刷發行
印　　　刷	中華彩色印刷股份有限公司
定　　　價	新台幣參佰元整

Author	Lee　Hwa　Lin
Publisher	Chin Chin Publishing Co., Ltd.
	4th fl., 125, Sung Chiang Rd.,
	Taipei, Taiwan, R.O.C.
	Tel:(02)2508-4331・2507-4902
Distributor	Wei-Chuan Publishing
	1455 Monterey Pass Rd., #110
	Monterey Park, CA91754, U.S.A.
	Tel :(323)2613880・2613878
	Fax:(323)2613299
Printer	China Color Printing Co.,Ltd
	Printed in Taiwan, R.O.C.
Copyright　Holder	Copyright © 1993
	By Wei-Chuan Cultural-Educational Foundation
	Sixth Printing, Sep., 2000
	ISBN 0-941676-31-5

序

味全文教基金會在民國八十年出版了第一本中國區域性的菜餚－－台灣菜，廣受讀者歡迎，給予我們很大的信心著手於搜集四川菜的資料。經過一年多的研究，並得川菜名廚莊賢三老師的指導，『四川菜』食譜終於出版了。

四川是中國文化的發源地之一，其位居中國西南方，有無數條河川流經省境，也造就了水流縱橫、草原寬廣、四周丘陵起伏的地理環境，這使四川米糧豐富，馬牛肥壯，魚蝦鮮美，擁有山珍海味的地利下，自古即被譽爲『天府之國』。

由於四川生產的烹調材料幾乎樣樣俱全，使當地人在烹調四川菜時，擅用各種山珍海味，其取材之廣，變化之多，堪稱一絕。又因自貢市所產的鹽，品質優良，使川菜在調味上又特別講究。

事實上，川味除了用鹽考究外，其他的味料要求也特別嚴格。一般而言，川味超過千種，例如乾燒、魚香、酸辣、麻辣、乾炒、怪味、椒麻、紅油、蒜泥、薑汁、陳皮、家常⋯等，烹飪者只要掌握其精髓稍予組合，更能自創出有獨特風味的菜色來，這在中國地方菜餚中，可謂首屈一指。

時至今日，川菜烹調的技術日新月異，在各方多年來不斷的改良下，早已使四川菜名揚海外，深受國外人士的喜愛，甚至可以說，有中國人的地方就有川菜館，使川菜成爲中國菜餚中的代表作之一。

有鑑於此，基金會特精心製作這本地方風味十足的食譜，希望把箇中精華與巧妙之處廣向國人介紹，進而推薦海外，發揚中國文化食的精髓。而此書得以順利推出，除了感謝味全家政班同仁不斷的研究，江文榮先生的精心拍攝外，尤其要謝謝川菜名廚莊賢三老師提供資料，並在製作過程中，親自擔任主廚之職，使此書完成傳承的理想。

林麗華

FOREWORD

Wei-Chuan Cultural Educational Foundation published its first Chinese regional cook book—Taiwanese cuisine in 1991. The book received wide acclaim and gave us great confidence in gathering information on Szechwan cuisine. After researching for more than a year, and under the supervision of the famous Szechwan chef, Mr. Hsien-San Chuang, the cook book of Szechwan cuisine is finally in print.

Szechwan is one of the places of origin for Chinese culture. It is located at the south-west of the Chinese mainland. Numerous rivers pass through the province. With fine irrigation systems it forms excellent grazing ground for cattle and produces tasty fish and shrimps from the surrounding rivers and lakes. With these natural geographic advantages, Szechwan is known as the "Country of Heaven".

Due to the fact that Szechwan produces all the ingredients necessary for cooking, it enabled the locals to use all types of materials when preparing Szechwan cuisine. At the same time, the provience produces the finest salt, which allows Szechwanese to be even more refined in their seasonings.

Besides making use of its unique salt , Szechwan cuisine also has strict requirements on all the other spices it uses. Generally speaking, there are more than one thousand flavors in Szechwan cuisine. For example: spicy dry braise, fish flavored, sour spicy, peppery spicy, dry fry, chili, garlic mash, ginger juice, dried orange peel,....ect.. A chef needs only to understand the essence of its cooking philosophy, and then you are free to use the different combinations to create your own unique dishes. Among all the Chinese regional cuisines, this is the special characteristics of Szechwan cuisine.

Today, cooking technics of Szechwan cuisine have modernized and improved to suit all palates. It is now known all over the world, and liked by many nationalities. It can be said that where is Chinese, there must be a Szechwan restaurant. Szechwan cuisine has become one of the most representative Chinese cuisines.

Wei-Chuan Foundation has made special efforts in producing this typical regional cook book in introducing the essence and the ingeniousness of Szechwan cooking. We would also like to take this opportunity to thank the staff of Wei-Chuan Cooking School for their continuous research, Mr. Wen-Ron Chiang for his skillful photography, and special thanks to Szechwan chef, Mr. Hsien-San Chuang for his information and personally presiding over all the cooking processes. All these efforts made this book possible.

Lee Hwa Lin

材料的前處理
Preparation of Special Food Material

花枝的處理
Squid

❶ 花枝去皮、頸。
❷ 去除內臟, 並用水洗淨。
❸ 花枝肉之內面, 每隔 0.3公分縱橫切入⅓深度, 使肉身作交叉片狀。
❹ 將片狀花枝切成 4 公分寬之條狀。

❶ Discard the neck part and peel off the skin.
❷ Discard the inner gut, and wash clean.
❸ Score inside every 0.3 cm and ⅓ deep, lengthwise and crosswise.
❹ Cut into 4 cm wide large strips.

花枝捲
Squid roll

❺ 每一條花枝肉再斜切成5×7公分之塊狀。

❺ Cut each strip into slanting 5 x 7 cm pieces.

花枝片
Squid slices

❻ 每一條花枝肉再切成2×4公分之塊狀。

❻ Cut each strip into 2 x 4 cm pieces.

蝦仁的處理
Shrimp

❶ 蝦用牙籤由背面挑去腸泥(若帶殼, 則先去殼)。
❷ 加太白粉、鹽, 輕輕拌洗。
❸ 用清水洗淨、瀝乾。

❶ Devine the shrimp with toothpick (must be shelled first).
❷ Rub gently with corn starch and salt.
❸ Rinse under water and drain.

蟹的清洗方法
Crab

❶ 將蟹的大螯剪斷, 或用筷子插入蟹的內臟, 待其斷氣。
❷ 將蟹殼洗刷乾淨。
❸ 掀起殼蓋, 去掉蓋內之腸泥及蟹鰓, 再洗淨即可。

❶ Snip off the big claws. Or pierce through with a chopstick.
❷ Brush clean the outer shell.
❸ Pull open the top shell, discard the inner dirt and gills. Wash clean.

魚翅的發法
Shark's Fin

❶ 加多量水浸泡一天。
❷ 剔除魚翅上之魚肉, 並洗淨。
❸ 加多量水及蔥、薑, 煮約3－5小時後待涼, 浸泡至魚翅變軟即可。

❶ Soak in plenty of water for one day.
❷ Trim off the first meat on the fin, wash clean.
❸ Boil in plenty of water, green onion and ginger for 3 to 5 hours; leave it cool. Soak again until softened.

海參的發法
Dried Sea Cucumber

❶ 乾海參洗淨, 泡水一天。
❷ 隔天換水, 煮開後熄火, 待水涼後換水再煮開, 如此一天3次, 連續發二天至軟。
❸ 由腹部剪開, 取出內臟洗淨, 加水煮開, 再發一天即可。

❶ Wash the dried sea cucumber, soak in water for one day.
❷ Place sea cucumber into new water and bring the water to one boil. When the water is cooled, change again to new water; bring to boil again. Repeat the process 3 times a day for 2 days, until the sea cucumber has softened.
❸ Snip open lengthwise and clean out the intestines. Cover it with water and bring to boil. Remove from heat and let it stand for one more day. Then it is ready for cooking.

木耳的發法
Dried Wood Ear

❶ 乾木耳泡水至軟。
❷ 洗淨。
❸ 去蒂。

❶ Soak the wood ears until softened.
❷ Wash clean.
❸ Cut off the stems.

蔥段的切法
Green Onion Sections

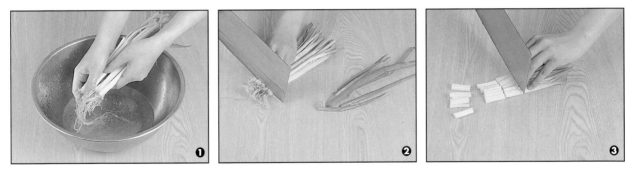

❶ 蔥洗淨。
❷ 去頭尾部分。
❸ 切成 3公分長段。

❶ Wash the green onion.
❷ Trim off the tops and roots.
❸ Cut into 3 cm long sections.

牛肉片的切法
Sliced Beef

❶ 牛肉洗淨。

❷ 放入冰庫中, 至半冷凍狀態再取出。

❸ 逆紋切斜片。

❶ Wash the beef clean.

❷ Put the beef in the freezer until half frozen.

❸ Cut into slanting slices against the grains.

腰花的處理
Kidney

❶ 豬腰去油脂, 以對半剖開。

❷ 切除內面之白筋網路。

❸ 腰花正面縱橫切刀, 再切成3×5公分之塊狀, 泡入冷水中。

❶ Trim off the fat, and cut to halves.

❷ Cut off inner white sinew membranes.

❸ Score the surface lengthwise and crosswise; then again cut into 3 x 5 cm pieces. Soak in cold water until cooking.

特殊材料的製作
Preparations of Special Cooking Materials

高湯
Stock

❶ 以豬、牛、雞的肉或骨頭入沸水中川燙。

❷ 再將肉或骨頭取出洗淨。

❸ 以另一鍋水燒開，再入洗淨的肉或骨頭，並加少許蔥、薑、酒，慢火熬煮出來的湯，謂之高湯。

❶ Parboil pork, beef, chicken or bones.

❷ Lift out and wash clean.

❸ Bring new clean water to boil, add in meat or bones together with a little green onion, ginger, and cooking wine. Simmer overlow heat until the soup is tasty.

糖色
Sugar Coloring

❶ 糖 4 大匙加水 2 大匙，以小火煮 5 分鐘至呈褐色。

❷ 再加半杯水，大火煮 3 分鐘至糖有黏性即成。

❶ Simmer 4T. sugar and 2T. water over low heat for 5 minutes until brown.

❷ Add in another ½C. water, boil over high heat for 3 minutes until the mixture turns to caramel.

紅油(辣油)
Red Oil (Chili Oil)

❶ 沙拉油燒至八分熱(180℃), 熄火入蔥、薑、花椒粒爆香至焦黃。
❷ 濾去蔥、薑、花椒粒。
❸ 辣椒粉以碗盛, 將爆香之沙拉油沖入其中即可。

備註: 沙拉油與辣椒粉之比例, 通常爲 5:1, 若不喜歡太辣, 可增加沙拉油
　　　之份量。

❶ Heat salad oil to 360°F (180°C). Turn off heat, add in green onion, ginger and Szechwan pepper corn; stir fry until fragant.
❷ Sieve off green onion, ginger and pepper corn.
❸ Place chili power in a bow, and pour hot oil over it.
※ The normal proportion of salad oil to chili power is 5:1 . If not so spicy desired, proportation of salad oil should be increased.

花椒鹽
Szechwan Pepper Salt

❶ 以乾鍋拌炒2大匙鹽, 至鹽呈微黃。
❷ 加1小匙花椒粉拌勻即成。

❶ Stir fry 2T. salt in a dry wok. Fry until salt turns slightly yellow.
❷ Mix evenly with 1t. Szechwan pepper power.

酒釀做法
Fermented Wine Rice

❶ 圓糯米 3 杯洗淨。
❷ 加水 3 杯煮熟。
❸ 打鬆吹涼。

❶ Wash 3C. glutinous rice clean.
❷ Cook rice with 3C. water until done.
❸ Loosen the rice and air it to cool.

❹ 酒麴, 取 1.5公克, 將酒麴拌入米飯中。
❺ 裝罐, 置於陰涼處使其醱酵。
❻ 酒釀成品。

❹ Mix rice with 1.5g. fermenting yeast.
❺ Put rice in a jar and leave it at a dark, cool place to ferment.
❻ Fermented wine rice.

鍋粑做法
Popped Rice Cake

❶ 圓糯米洗淨, 以糯米十分之九的水分略爲浸泡。
❷ 入電鍋煮熟即爲糯米飯。
❸ 將糯米飯鋪於烤盤上。
❹ 將米飯壓平壓緊。
❺ 入烤箱中, 以70℃烤至米粒全乾, 即可起出切塊, 即爲鍋粑。

❶ Wash short grain glutinous rice clean. Soak in proportion of 1 part rice to 9/10 water.
❷ Steam in rice cooker.
❸ Spread glutinous rice over a baking sheet.
❹ Press on the rice to make it even and tight.
❺ Bake in 158°F(70°C) oven until rice is all dried out. Remove and cut into serving squares to be popped rice cakes.

重量換算表
Measure Equivalents

1磅=454公克 =16盎士   1盎士=28.4公克

1lb.=454gm (454g.) =16oz.   1oz.=28.4gm (28.4g.)

烹調的方法
Guide to Cooking Terms

川燙
Parboil

❶ 鍋水以大火煮沸。
❷ 放入材料再煮沸,隨即撈起。
❸ 漂冷水。

❶ Bring water to boil over high heat.
❷ Add in materials and bring to boil once again.
   Quickly lift out.
❸ Rinse under cold water.

❶ 將食物泡入熱油內(五分熱 120℃),食物剛熱即刻撈出, 時間不可過長,
   謂之過油。

❶ Soak the cooking materials into hot oil (240°F/120°C),
   lift out as soon as they are cooked. It should be done
   in a minimum time required.

過油
Hot Oil Soaking

量器説明
Table of Measurements

1杯=236c.c=1 cup (1C.)
1大匙=1湯匙=15c.c=1 Tablespoon (1T.)
1小匙=1茶匙=5c.c=1 Teaspoon (1t.)

目錄 Contents

干燒青蟹
Spicy Crab

800g.(1¾lb.)..........................Crab
1C..Flour

1 ⎡ 2T.each Minced green onion,
　　　 minced garlic,
　　⎣ minced ginger

2 ⎡ ¾C.Catchup
　　 ½C.Water
　　 2T.Fermented wine rice
　　 2t.Sugar
　　⎣ 1t.Hot soy bean paste

青蟹...........800公克　　麵粉...............1杯

1 ⎡ 蔥末、蒜末、薑
　　⎣ 末　　各2大匙

2 ⎡ 蕃茄醬　¾杯
　　 水　　　½杯
　　 酒釀　　2大匙
　　 糖　　　2小匙
　　⎣ 辣豆瓣醬 1小匙

❶ 青蟹洗淨剁成塊狀，並沾上麵粉。
❷ 鍋熱入油 7 杯燒至七分熱（160℃），入青蟹炸至金黃色撈起瀝油。
❸ 鍋內留油 3 大匙，爆香**1**料，再入蟹塊及**2**料煮開即可。

❶ Wash the crab and cut it into serving pieces; dredge with flour.
❷ Heat the wok, add 7C. oil and heat to 320°F (160°C). Deep fry the crab until golden and drain.
❸ Keep 3T. oil in the wok and stir fry **1** until fragant. Add in the crab and **2** ; cook until boil and serve.

螃蟹(800公克)..2隻　　高湯...............½杯
麵粉...............3大匙　　蔥末、薑末 各1大匙
麻油...............1小匙

1 ⎡ 醬油　　1½大匙
　　 酒、甜麵醬
　　　　　各1大匙
　　⎣ 糖　　　½大匙

2 ⎡ 水　　　2小匙
　　⎣ 太白粉　1小匙

❶ 螃蟹洗淨，切塊(圖1)沾麵粉(圖2)備炸。
❷ 鍋熱入油 3 杯燒至七分熱（160℃），放入蟹塊炸至金黃色(圖3)，即撈出瀝油。
❸ 鍋內留油 3 大匙，將蔥、薑炒香，隨入**1**料、蟹塊及高湯燒至汁剩下一半時，以**2**料勾芡，最後淋熱油½大匙及麻油 1 小匙即可。

醬爆青蟹
Crab with Bean Paste Sauce

| 青蟹(約800公克)2隻 | 蛋白 .... 3個 | 800g.(1¾lb.) .... Crab |
| 雞油 .... 2大匙 | 薑末、蔥末 各1大匙 | 3 .... Egg white |

1
[水 ½杯
 酒 ½大匙
 鹽 ½小匙
 胡椒粉 ¼小匙]

2
[水 1大匙
 太白粉 ½大匙]

1T.each...
Minced green onion,minced ginger
2T. .... Chicken fat

1
[½C.Water
 ½T.Cooking wine
 ½t.Salt
 ¼t.Pepper]

2
[1T.Water
 ½T.Corn starch]

❶ 蛋白先打發備用。
❷ 蟹洗淨, 每隻切成6 - 8塊, 鍋熱入油½杯燒至六分熱(140℃), 將蟹煎至兩面稍黃, 入蔥、薑及**1**料, 蓋上鍋蓋燜煮3分鐘, 以**2**料勾茨, 入蛋白拌勻, 再淋上雞油即可。

❶ Beat the egg whites.
❷ Wash the crab, cut into 6 - 8 pieces per crab. Heat the wok, add ½C. oil; heat to 284°F (140°C). Fry the crab to slightly golden; stir in green onion, ginger, and **1**. Cover and braise for 3 minutes. Thicken with **2**, mix in egg whites evenly; sprinkle on chicken fat and serve.

800g.(1¾lb.) .... Crab
3T. .... Flour
1T.each...
Minced green onion,minced ginger
1t. .... Sesame oil
½C. .... Stock

1
[1½T.Soy sauce
 1T.each Cooking wine,
      sweet soy bean paste
 ½T.Sugar]

2
[2t.Water
 1t.Corn starch]

❶ Wash the crab and cut into serving pieces (illus. 1). Dredge in flour (illus. 2).
❷ Heat the wok, add in 3C. oil; heat to 320°F (160°C). Deep fry the crab until golden (illus. 3).
❸ Keep 3T. oil in the wok, stir fry green onion and ginger until fragant. Add in **1**, crab pieces and stcok, boil until the sauce reduce to half. Thicken with **2**, sprinkle on ½T. hot oil and sesame oil; serve.

豆豉鯧魚
Pomfret with Black Bean Sauce

600g.(1⅓lb.) .... Pomfret
1 sheet .... Pork fat membrane

1
- 1T. Cooking wine
- ¼t. Salt

2
- 4T. Minced green onion
- 3T.each Minced hot red pepper, fermented black soy bean
- 2½T. Minced ginger
- 2T.each Soy sauce, pork fat

鯧魚 .... 600公克　網油 1張

1
- 酒　　　　1大匙
- 鹽　　　　¼小匙

2
- 蔥末　　　4大匙
- 辣椒末、豆豉　各3大匙
- 薑末　　2½大匙
- 醬油、豬油　各2大匙

❶ 鯧魚洗淨, 在表面劃數刀後先川燙, 瀝乾後在表面塗抹**1**料。
❷ **2**料調勻鋪於魚身上, 再以網油包起來, 入鍋大火蒸12分鐘即可。

❶ Clean the pomfret and cut few diagonal slits on the skin. Parboil slightly and drain. Marinate with **1** .
❷ Mix **2** evenly and spread over the surface; wrap pork fat membrane over the fish. Steam over high heat for 12 minutes, and serve.
※ One table spoon of lard may be used in stead of pork fat membrane.

石斑魚肉 ... 600公克
蔥末 3大匙
白醋 1小匙

1
- 辣豆瓣醬、薑末、蒜末 各2大匙
- 酒釀　　　1大匙

2
- 水　　　1½杯
- 糖　　　½大匙
- 鹽　　　½小匙
- 味精　　⅛小匙

3
- 水　　　2大匙
- 太白粉　1大匙

❶ 魚洗淨去骨(圖1)後, 切成 3×4 公分片狀(圖2)備用。
❷ 油6杯燒至七分熱(160℃), 入魚塊炸至金黃色(圖3)撈起。
❸ 留油⅓杯炒香**1**料, 放入魚片及**2**料燒約10分鐘, 並以**3**料勾芡灑上蔥末及醋即可。

豆瓣斑魚片
Rock Cod Fillet with Hot Bean Sauce

椒鹽鯧魚
Fried Pomfret with Seasoned Salt

鯧魚 ....300公克　麻油 2大匙
┌ 蔥　　　2段　　┌ 蔥末　　1大匙
│ 薑　　　3片　 **2**┤ 鹽　　　½小匙
1┤ 鹽　　½小匙　　└ 花椒粉　¼小匙
│ 酒、胡椒粉
└　　　　各¼小匙

300g.(10⅔oz.) ....Pomfret
2T. ....Sesame oil
1┌ 2 sections Green onion
　│ 3 slices Ginger
　│ ½t.Salt
　└ ¼t.each Cooking wine, pepper
2┌ 1T.Minced green onion
　│ ½t.Salt
　└ ¼t.Szechwan pepper powder

● 鯧魚洗淨兩面切交叉花刀, 抹上**1**料醃。
● 鍋燒熱, 入油½杯燒至七分熱(160℃), 將
魚入鍋煎至呈金黃色, 取出置盤灑上**2**料,
再淋上熱麻油即可。

● Wash and clean the fish. Cut diagonal slits over the skin on both sides. Marinate with **1** .
● Heat the wok, add ½C. oil, heat to 320°F (160°C). Fry the fish to golden on both sides. Place it on a platter and sprinkle on **2** . Then sprinkle hot sesame oil over and serve.

00g.(1⅓lb.) .... Rock Cod Fillet
T. .... Minced green onion
. ... White vinegar

1┌ 2T.each Hot soy bean poaste,
　│　　minced ginger, minced
　│　　garlic
　└ 1T.Fermented wine rice
2┌ 1½C.Water
　│ ½T.Sugar
　└ ½t.Salt
3┌ 2T.Water
　└ 1T.Corn starch

● Wash and bone (illus. 1) the fillets. Cut into 3x4 cm pieces (illus. 2).
● Heat the wok, add in 6C. oil. Heat to 320°F (160°C),fry the fish until golden (illus. 3), and drain.
● Keep ⅓C. oil in the wok and stir fry **1** until fragant. Add in the fish and **2** ; cook for 10 minutes. Thicken with **3** . Sprinkle on green onion and vinegar. Serve.

豆瓣魚
Braised Carp with Hot Bean Paste

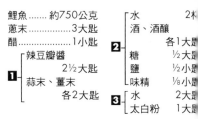

鯉魚 約750公克			水	2杯
蔥末 3大匙			酒、酒釀	
醋 1小匙		**2**	各1大匙	
			糖	½大匙
1	辣豆瓣醬		鹽	½小匙
	2½大匙		味精	⅛小匙
	蒜末、薑末			
	各2大匙		**3** 水	2大匙
			太白粉	1大匙

❶ 魚洗淨,在魚背肉厚處劃刀(圖1),煮時料
易入味且易熟。

❷ 鍋熱入油 6 杯燒至八分熱(180℃),提起魚
尾順鍋邊(圖2)滑入鍋中,將兩面炸黃,撈
起備用。

❸ 留油⅓杯炒香**1**料,放入魚(圖3)及**2**料燒
約10分鐘,並以**3**料勾芡,灑上蔥末及醋即
可。

750g.(1⅔lb) .... Car
3T. .... Minced green onio
1t. .... Vineg

1 ⎡ 2½T.Hot soy bean paste
    ⎣ 2T.each Minced garlic,
                 minced ginger

2 ⎡ 2C.Water
    │ 1T.each Cooking wine, fermented
                 wine rice
    │ ½T.Sugar
    ⎣ ½t.Salt

3 ⎡ 2T.Water
    ⎣ 1T.Corn starch

❶ Wash and clean the fish. Cut diagonal slits at the thick parts (illus. 1), for easier cooking and tastier.

❷ Heat the wok, add 6C. oil. Heat to 356°F (180°C). Lift the fish by the tail and slide into the wok (illus. 2). Fry until golden on both sides, and remove.

❸ Keep ⅓C. oil in the wok and stir fry **1** until fragant. Add in the fish (illus. 3) and **2**; cook for about 10 minutes. Thicken with **3** . Sprinkle on green onion and vinegar; and serve.

糖醋魚
Sweet and Sour Fish

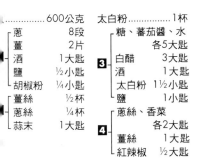

...............600公克		太白粉.................1杯
蔥	8段	糖、蕃茄醬、水
薑	2片	各5大匙
1 酒	1大匙	**3** 白醋 3大匙
鹽	½小匙	酒 1大匙
胡椒粉	¼小匙	太白粉 1½小匙
薑絲	½杯	鹽 1小匙
蔥絲	¼杯	蔥絲、香菜
蒜末	1大匙	各2大匙
		4 薑絲 1大匙
		紅辣椒 ½大匙

● 魚身兩面切斜刀(圖1)，以**1**料抹勻魚身(圖2)醃30分鐘,炸時再沾裹太白粉(圖3)。
● 鍋熱入油6杯燒至八分熱(約180℃),中火將魚炸約10分鐘撈出。
● 鍋內留油半杯,入**2**料炒香,再入**3**料煮開,並加1大匙油淋在魚身上,再灑上**4**料即可。

whole..Fish		
C. ....Corn Starch		
8 sections	Green onion	
2 slices	Ginger	
1T.	Cooking wine	
½t.	Salt	
¼t.	Pepper	
½C.	Shredded ginger	
¼C.	Shredded green onion	
1T.	Minced garlic	
5T.each	Sugar, catchup, water	
3T.	White vinegar	
1T.	Cooking wine	
1½t.	Corn starch	
½t.	Salt	
2T.each	Shredded green onion,coriander	
1T.	Shredded ginger	
½T.	Red pepper	

❶ Cut few diagonal slits on both sides of the fish (illus. 1). Marinate with **1** (illus. 2) for 30 minutes. Dredge in flour before frying (illus. 3).
❷ Heat the wok, add 6C. oil. Heat to 356°F (180°C). Fry the fish for 10 minutes and drain.
❸ Keep ½C. oil in the wok, stir fry **2** until fragant. Add in **3** to boil. Pour 1T. oil over the fish and sprinkle on **4**. Serve.

豆酥鱈魚
Halibut with Crispy Bean Sauce

鱈魚 .... 600公克　　絞肉 110公克
白豆酥(約90公克)　　辣豆瓣醬(圖2)、麻
(圖1) .... 1個　　油 各1大匙
蔥末 .... ½大匙

1 ┌ 蔥　　　　6段　　**2** ┌ 糖　　　½小匙
　　├ 薑　　　　4片　　　　└ 味精　　¼小匙
　　├ 酒　　　1大匙
　　└ 鹽、胡椒粉
　　　　　　各¼小匙

❶ 鱈魚洗淨加**1**料醃30分鐘,再入蒸籠蒸12分鐘取出,倒出水份備用。
❷ 鍋熱入油4大匙,炒熟絞肉,入豆酥及**2**料炒至豆酥呈酥狀(圖3)時,再入辣豆瓣醬拌勻,待豆酥呈濕狀時,即入蔥末、麻油,拌炒均勻淋在魚上即可。

600g.(1⅓lb.) .... Halibut
110g.(4oz.) .... Minced pork
90g.(3⅕oz.) ....
.... Beige fermented beans (illus. 1)
1T.each..
Hot soy bean paste(illus. 2), sesame oil
½T...................... Minced green onion

1 ┌ 6 sections Green onion
　　├ 4 slices Ginger
　　├ 1T.Cooking wine
　　└ ¼t.each Salt, pepper
2 ½t.Sugar

❶ Clean the fish and marinate in **1** for 30 minutes. Steam for 12 minutes; remove and drain.
❷ Heat the wok, add 4T. oil. Stir fry the pork until done, add in beans and **2** ; fry until beans are crispy (illus. 3). Then mix in hot bean paste evenly. When the mixture looks wet, add in minced green onion and sesame oil. Mix thoroughly and spread over the fish; and Serve.

鯰魚 .... 600公克　大蒜(去皮) 16顆
蔥末 .... 3大匙　蒜苗、麻油.各1大匙
酒 .... ½大匙　薑末 1小匙

1
┌ 水　　　　1杯
│ 醬油　　　2大匙
│ 鎮江醋　　½大匙
│ 糖　　　　2小匙
│ 味精、胡椒粉
└ 　　　　各¼小匙

2
┌ 水　　　½大匙
└ 太白粉　1小匙

❶ 鯰魚洗淨瀝乾,切成 3 公分之塊狀(圖 1)。
　蒜苗先將蒜白部份斜切(圖 2), 蒜葉切絲(圖 3)備用。

❷ 鍋熱入油 3 大匙燒熱, 入大蒜炒香, 續入蒜
　白、薑末及魚煎約 1 分鐘, 入酒及**1**料, 蓋
　鍋以小火燜煮約10分鐘, 用**2**料勾芡, 最後
　加麻油拌勻, 灑上蒜葉、蔥末盛盤即可。

600g.(1⅓lb.) .... Cat fish
16 .... Garlic clove (skinned)
3T. .... Minced green onion
1T.each .... Sesame oil, garlic leek
½T. .... Cooking wine
1t. .... Minced ginger

1
┌ 1C.Water
│ 2T.Soy sauce
│ ½T.Black vinegar
│ 2t.Sugar
└ ¼t.Pepper

2
┌ ½T.Water
└ 1t.Corn Starch

❶ Wash and drain the fish, cut into 3 cm pieces (illus. 1). Cut the white part of the garlic leek into diagonal slices (illus. 2), and shred the green leaves (illus. 3).

❷ Heat the wok, add 3T. oil. Heat to hot and stir fry minced garlic to fragant. Add in white parts of the garlic leek, ginger and fish; fry for 1 minute. Then add in wine and **1** . Cover and braised over low heat for 10 minutes. Thicken with **2** . Pour sesame oil over the fish and sprinkle on minced green onion and shredded green garlic leek. Serve.

生炒鮮貝
Stir Fried Fresh Scallop

230g.(8oz.) .... Fresh scallop slices
90g.(3⅕oz.) .... Celery slices
½C. .... Stock
4 sections .... Green onion
1T.each .... Garlic
slices, red pepper slices, chicken fat

1 ½T.Cooking wine
  ½t.Salt
2 1T.Water
  ½T.Corn starch

鮮干貝片 ... 230公克		西芹片 90公克	
高湯 .... ½杯		紅辣椒片、蒜片、	
蔥 4段		雞油 各1大匙	

1 酒 ½大匙
  鹽 ½小匙
  味精 ⅛小匙
2 水 1大匙
  太白粉 ½大匙

❶ 水7杯煮開,入干貝及西芹,撈出漂冷水瀝
 乾備用。
❷ 鍋熱入油2大匙,爆香蔥段、蒜片、辣椒
 片,再入高湯、干貝、西芹與**1**料,煮開後
 以**2**料勾芡,起鍋後淋上雞油即可。

❶ Bring 7C. water to boil, parboil the scallop and celery. Remove and rinse under cold water; drain.
❷ Heat the wok, add 2T. oil, stir fry green onion, garlic and red pepper until fragant. Add in stock, scallop, celery and **1** until boil. Thicken with **2** . Remove to a platter, sprinkle on chicken fat and serve.

鮮干貝 350公克		**1** 薑 4片	
洋蔥 150公克		蒜片 1大匙	
青椒 100公克		**2** 水 ½杯	
洋菇 40公克		酒、醬油	
紅辣椒 2條		各1大匙	

2 麻油、太白粉
  各1小匙
  胡椒粉 ½小匙
  鹽、味精
  各¼小匙

❶ 鮮貝、洋蔥、青椒切片,辣椒去籽(圖1)切
 片(圖2)備用。
❷ 鐵板燒熱備用。
❸ 油3杯燒至八分熱(180℃),將洋蔥、青椒
 、洋菇、紅辣椒過油盛於鐵板上,鮮貝續
 入鍋中泡油,隨即撈起置於鐵板上。
❹ 留油1大匙燒熱,入**1**料爆香,再入**2**料拌
 勻,盛於鐵板上即可。
※ 鐵板蝦仁:將干貝改成蝦仁,再加1⅓大
  匙太白粉及¼小匙鹽醃拌均勻,
  其餘材料及做法與鐵板干貝同
  。

鐵板干貝
Scallop on Sizzling Plate

生蚵 300公克	甘薯粉 150公克	300g.(10⅔oz.)............ Fresh oyster
蕃茄醬或花椒鹽		150g.(5⅓oz.) Sweet-potato powder
...................2大匙		2T............ Catchup or seasoned salt

❶ 將生蚵洗淨放入滾水中川燙，撈起瀝乾水份，入甘薯粉拌勻，使每粒生蚵沾滿甘薯粉。

❷ 鍋熱入油4杯燒至七分熱(160℃)，將生蚵入鍋炸至微黃即可盛盤，食用時沾蕃茄醬或花椒鹽。

❶ Wash and parboil the oysters. Drain and mix in sweet-potato powder evenly. Each oyster must be coated.

❷ Heat the wok, add 4C. oil. Heat to 320°F (160°C), fry the oysters to slightly golden. Remove and serve with catchup or seasoned salt.

50g.(12⅓oz.) .... Fresh scallop	
50g.(5⅓oz.) ....Onion	
00g.(3½oz.) .... Green pepper	
0g.(1⅖oz.) ....Mushroom	
.... Red pepper	

❶ [4 slices Ginger
[1T.Garlic slices
❷ [½C.Water
1T.each Cooking wine, soy sauce
1t.each Sesame oil, corn starch
½t.Pepper
¼t.Salt

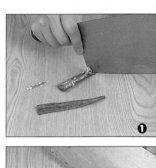

❶ Cut scallop, onion and green pepper into serving slices. Remove the seeds (illus. 1) in the red pepper, and cut into slices (illus. 2).

❷ Heat the hot plate.

❸ Heat the wok, add 3C. oil. Heat to 356°F (180°C). Soak onion, green pepper, mushroom and red pepper in the hot oil; and immediately drain and remove onto the hot plate. Then soak the scallop into the hot oil, also immediately drain and place onto the hot plate.

❹ Keep 1T. oil in the wok, stir fry **❶** until fragant. Add in **❷** evenly. Remove and pour over scallop.

※ Shrimp on Sizzling Plate: Use shrimp instead of scallop. Marinate in 1⅓T. corn starch and ¼t. salt. The rest of materials and methods is the same as above.

干燒蝦仁
Spicy Shrimp

300g.(10⅔oz.)........ Shelled shrimp

1
- 1T.Corn starch
- ½ Egg white
- ¼t.Salt

2
- ½T.each Minced green onion, minced garlic, minced ginger

3
- 2T.Catchup
- ½T.Fermented wine rice
- 1t.Sugar
- ½t.Hot soy bean paste

4
- 1T.Water
- ½T.Corn starch

蝦仁 300公克

1
- 太白粉　　1大匙
- 蛋白　　　½個
- 鹽　　　　¼小匙

2
- 蔥末、蒜末、薑末　各½大匙

3
- 蕃茄醬　　2大匙
- 酒釀　　　½大匙
- 糖　　　　1小匙
- 辣豆瓣醬　½小匙

4
- 水　　　　1大匙
- 太白粉　　½大匙

❶ 蝦仁洗淨瀝乾，入 **1** 料拌勻甩打數下，冰涼備用。
❷ 鍋熱入油 3 杯燒至七分熱（160℃），入蝦仁炸熟取出，鍋內留油 3 大匙，入 **2** 料炒香再入 **3** 料及蝦仁拌炒均勻，再以 **4** 料勾芡即可。

❶ Wash and drain the shrimps. Mix in **1** and beat the mixture a few times. Chill.
❷ Heat the wok, add 3C. oil. Heat to 320°F (160°C), fry the shrimp until cooked. Keep 3T. oil in the wok, stir fry **2** until fragant. Add in **3** and shrimp, stir fry thoroughly. Thicken with **4** and serve.

蝦仁 225公克
荸薺 38公克
肥肉 38公克
麵包粉 1杯
鹽 .... ¼小匙
巴西利梗 ....少許

1
- 蛋白　　　½個
- 太白粉　　½大匙
- 薑酒汁　　½小匙
- 鹽　　　　¼小匙
- 味精、胡椒粉　各⅛小匙

❶ 荸薺及肥肉剁碎備用，蝦仁洗淨瀝乾，加鹽¼小匙拌勻，用刀面將蝦仁壓碎後，剁成蝦泥。
❷ 蝦泥加 **1** 料拌勻，並順同一方向攪拌至有黏性，再加入荸薺、肥肉拌勻即爲蝦絨。
❸ 用手將蝦絨擠成12個蝦丸(圖1)，沾麵包粉(圖2)，再捏成果子狀，並以巴西利梗裝飾(圖3)，即爲蝦果。
❹ 鍋熱入油 4 杯燒至六分熱（140℃），將蝦果入鍋，用小火炸至蝦果浮出，並呈金黃色即可。
※ 百角蝦球：將麵包粉改成土司丁，其他材料及做法與脆皮蝦果相同。

脆皮蝦果
Crispy Shrimp Fruit

蝦仁豆腐
Bean Curd with Shrimp

蝦仁 150公克
豆腐 1½塊
毛豆 2大匙
薑末 1大匙
蔥 4段

2
高湯 1½杯
鹽 .... ½小匙
胡椒粉、味精
.... 各¼小匙

3
太白粉、水
.... 各1½大匙

1
蛋白 .... ¼個
太白粉 1小匙
鹽 .... ¼小匙

150g.(5⅓oz.) .... Shelled shrimp
1½ ....Bean curd
2T. .... Fresh soy bean
1T. ....Minced ginger
4 sections .... Green onion

1
¼ Egg white
1t. Corn starch
¼t. Salt

2
1½C. Stock
½t. Salt
¼t. Pepper

3 1½T. each Water, corn starch

❶ 蝦仁洗淨, 入**1**料醃5分鐘備用。
❷ 豆腐切丁, 鍋熱入油1杯燒至五分熱(120
℃), 入蝦仁過油, 備用。
❸ 鍋內留油3大匙, 爆香蔥、薑, 入豆腐、毛
豆及**2**料燒煮3分鐘, 最後拌入蝦仁, 以**3**
料勾芡即可。

❶ Clean the shrimp and marinate in **1** for 5 minutes.
❷ Dice the bean curd. Heat the wok, add 1C. oil. Heat to 248°F (120°C). Soak the shrimp in hot oil and quickly lift out.
❸ Keep 3T. oil in the wok, stir fry green onion and ginger until fragant. Add in bean curd, fresh soy bean and **2** ; cook for 3 minutes. Mix in the shrimp, thicken with **3** and serve.

225g.(8oz.) .... Shelled shrimp
38g.(1⅓oz.) .... Water chestnut
38g.(1⅓oz.) .... Pork fat
1C. .... Bread crumb
¼t. .... Salt
Few stems .... Parsley stem

1
½ Egg white
½T. Corn starch
½t. Ginger wine juice
¼t. Salt
⅛t. Pepper

❶ Chop both water chestnut and pork very fine. Wash and drain shrimp, mix with ¼t. salt evenly; crash shrimp with the back of a knife, and then chop to shrimp paste.
❷ Mix shrimp paste with **1** evenly, and beat clockwise until the mixture sticky. Add in water chestnut and pork, mix thoroughly.
❸ Squeeze shrimp mixture to form 12 shrimp balls with hands (illus. 1). Dip in bread crumb (illus. 2), form balls into fruit shapes, and decorate with parsley stems (illus. 3) to resemble fruits.
❹ Heat the wok, add 4C. oil, and heat to 284°F (140°C). Deep fry shrimp fruit until floats and golden.
※ Shrimp Balls with Hundred Corners : Substitute bread crumb with diced toast bread. Other materials and methods are same as above.

宮保蝦仁
Kun–Pao Shrimp

蝦仁 300公克

1
- 乾辣椒　　3/4杯
- 花椒粒(圖1)
- 　　　　　1小匙

2
- 蔥　　　　4段
- 薑末　　　2小匙

3
- 蛋白　　　1個
- 太白粉　　1大匙
- 鹽　　　　1/8小匙

4
- 醬油　　　2大匙
- 酒、糖、糖色、
- 白醋、水
- 　　　各1大匙
- 太白粉、麻油
- 　　　各1/2小匙

❶ 蝦仁洗淨瀝乾水分後，以**3**料醃拌10分鐘，鍋熱入油3杯燒至五分熱(約120℃)，入蝦仁過油備用。
❷ 乾辣椒切段(圖2)、去籽(圖3)備用。
❸ 鍋內留油3大匙，入**1**料炒香，再入**2**料爆香，隨即入蝦仁與**4**料，拌炒均勻即可。
※ 宮保花枝：將宮保蝦仁之蝦仁改爲花枝淨肉300公克，並於**2**料中加入蒜末2小匙，其餘材料及做法與宮保蝦仁同。

300g.(10 2/3 oz.)........... Shelled shrimp

1
- 3/4 C. Dried red pepper
- 1t. Szechwan peppercorn (illus. 1)

2
- 4 sections Green onion
- 2t. Minced ginger

3
- 1 Egg white
- 1T. Corn starch
- 1/8 t. Salt

4
- 2T. Soy sauce
- 1T. each Cooking wine, sugar, sugar coloring, white vinegar, water
- 1/2 t. each Corn starch, sesame oil

❶ Wash and drain the shrimp. Marinate in **3** for 10 minutes. Heat the wok, add 3 C. oil. Heat to 248°F (120°C), soak the shrimp in the hot oil and quickly lift out.
❷ Cut the dried red peppers (illus 2) into shorter sections (illus 3).
❸ Heat 3T. oil in the wok, stir fry **1** until fragant; add in **2** . Then add in shrimp and **4** . Mix well and serve.
※ Kun-Pao Squid: Use squid instead of shrimp, and add 2t. minced garlic into **2** . The rest of the materials and the methods remains the same as above.

青豆蝦仁
Shrimp with Green Peas

蝦仁 200公克
豌豆仁 150公克
高湯 .... ½杯
蔥 4段
薑 3片
麻油 1小匙

1
蛋白 ½個
太白粉 1大匙
酒 ½小匙
鹽 ¼小匙

2
糖、酒 各1大匙
白醋 ½小匙
胡椒粉、鹽
各¼小匙
味精 ⅛小匙

3
太白粉、水
各1小匙

❶ 蝦仁洗淨瀝乾水份，加**1**料醃10分鐘備用。

❷ 豌豆仁以開水燙熟，撈出漂冷水備用。

❸ 鍋熱入油4杯燒至六分熱(140℃)，入蝦仁泡熟，取出瀝乾油。

❹ 鍋中留油3大匙，入蔥、薑爆香，入**2**料、高湯、蝦仁及豌豆仁快速拌炒均勻，再以**3**料勾芡並淋上麻油即可。

※ 磨菇蝦仁：將豌豆仁改成洋菇200公克，並切成1公分立方，蔥段切成末，其餘材料及做法均與青豆蝦仁同。

200g.(7oz.) .... Shelled shrimp
150g.(5⅓oz.) .... Green pea
4 sections .... Green onion
3 slices .... Ginger
½C. .... Stock
1t. .... Sesame oil

1
½ Egg white
1T. Corn starch
½t. Cooking wine
¼t. Salt

2
1T. each Sugar, cooking wine
¼t. each Salt, pepper
½t. White vinegar

3 ¼T. Corn starch, water

❶ Wash and drain shrimp. Marinate in **1** for 10 minutes.

❷ Boil the peas and rinse under cold water. Drain.

❸ Heat the wok, add 4C. oil. Heat to 284°F (140°C), soak shrimp in the hot oil until cooked. Lift out and drain.

❹ Keep 3T. oil in the wok, stir fry green onion, and ginger until fragant. Add in **2**, stock, shrimp and peas, stir fry quickly. Thickenly with **3**. Sprinkle on sesame oil and serve.

※ Shrimp with Mushroom: Use 200g.(7oz.) mushroom instead of green pea. Cut mushroom into 1 cm cubes, and chop green onion sections. The rest of materials and methods remains the same as above.

蝦仁	230公克		蛋白	½個
肥肉	38公克		太白粉	½大匙
荸薺	38公克	**1**	薑酒汁	½小匙
蛋	3個		鹽	¼小匙
網油	2張		胡椒粉	⅛小匙
黑芝麻	½杯			
太白粉	少許			

❶ 荸薺及肥肉剁碎,蛋打均勻,備用。

❷ 蝦仁洗淨瀝乾,加鹽¼小匙拌勻,再用刀背將蝦仁壓碎後,再剁成蝦泥。

❸ 將蝦泥加**1**料拌勻,順同一方向攪拌至有黏性,約3分鐘再加入荸薺、肥肉拌勻成蝦絨。

❹ 蝦絨用網油(圖1)包捲成直徑約2公分長條狀,只裹2圈,並於合口處灑些太白粉(圖2)以利黏合,入鍋蒸約5分鐘,取出將頭尾切整齊(圖3),並每隔3公分切一段,將切口兩端沾上蛋汁,再沾黑芝麻備用。

❺ 鍋熱入油6杯燒至七分熱(160℃)入蝦捲炸至金黃色即可。

230g.(8oz.)	Shelled shrimp
38g.(1⅓oz.)	Pork bacon
38g.(1⅓oz.)	Water chestnut
3	Egg
2 sheet	Pork fat membrane
½C.	Black Sesame
dash	Corn starch

	½ Egg white	
	½T.Corn starch	
1	½t.Ginger wine juice	
	¼t.Salt	
	⅛t.Pepper	

❶ Mince water chestnut and pork bacon. Beat the eggs.

❷ Wash and drain the shrimps, mix with ¼t. salt. Crash the shrimps with the back of knife, and chop to paste.

❸ Mix shrimp past with **1** , whip clock-wise for 3 minutes until sticky. Then add in water chestnut and pork bacon to be shrimp mixtue.

❹ Wrap shrimp mixtue with pork fat membrane into 2 cm diameter long rolls (illus. 1), wrap only two layers around. Seal the opening with corn starch (illus. 2). Steam for 5 minutes. Trim the ends even (illus. 3), cut every 3 cm; dip the ends with egg and black sesame.

❺ Heat the wok, add 6C. oil. Heat to 320°F (160°C), fry the shrimp rolls until golden.

椒麻蝦仁
Shrimp with Chili Sauce

蝦仁 230公克
粉皮 5張

2	
蛋白	½個
太白粉	1小匙
鹽、酒 各½小匙	

2	
蔥末	½杯
開水	2大匙
薑末、醬油	
	各1大匙
麻油、花椒粉	
	各½大匙
白醋、辣油	
	各1小匙

❶ 蝦仁洗淨瀝乾，入 **1** 料醃約10分鐘，粉皮切成條狀備用(圖1)。

❷ 水7杯煮開，陸續放入蝦仁、粉皮燙熟撈出(圖2)瀝乾，將蝦仁置於粉皮上，並淋上 **2** 料即可。

※ 椒麻腰片：將蝦仁改為豬腰500公克，並將豬腰除去內筋切斜薄片，**1** 料改為蔥1支、薑1片、酒、鹽各½小匙，並與腰片一起川燙，其餘材料及做法與椒麻蝦仁同。

230g.(8¹⁄₁₀oz.) ....Shelled Shrimp
.... Green bean sheet

1	
1t.Corn starch	
½t.each Salt,cooking wine	
½ Egg white	

2	
½C.Minced green onion	
2T.Hot water	
1T.each Minced ginger,soy sauce	
½T.each Sesame oil, Szechwan	
pepper powder	
1t.each White vinegar, chili oil	

❶ Wash and dry shrimp; marinate with **1** for about 10 minutes. Cut green bean sheet into long strips (illus. 1).

❷ Bring 7C. water to boil, parboil shrimp and green bean sheet (illus. 2); lift out and drain. Place shrimp on top of green bean sheet, pour over **2** and serve.

※ Kidney with Chili Sauce: Substitute shrimp with 500g.(1¹⁄₅lb.) kidney, trim off inner sinew, and cut into slanting thin slices. Marinate kidney slices with 1 green onion, 1 slice ginger, ½t. each salt and cooking wine; parboil them all together. The rest remains the same above.

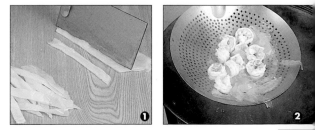

鍋粑蝦仁
Sizzling Rice Cake with Shrimps

蝦仁	225公克		水或高湯　　2杯
鍋粑	120公克		蕃茄醬　　3大匙
青豆仁	50公克	**2**	糖　　　　1大匙
蔥	4段		醬油　　½大匙
薑	3片		鹽　　　¼小匙
麻油	1大匙	**3**	太白粉、水
1 蛋白　　½個			各2大匙
太白粉　2小匙			
鹽　　¼小匙			

❶ 洗淨蝦仁, 拭乾水份, 入**1**料拌勻醃約20分鐘, 鍋粑切成3公分之四方塊 (圖1)。

❷ 鍋熱入油6杯燒至七分熱(160℃), 入鍋粑炸至金黃色(圖2), 盛於大盤內備用。

❸ 蝦仁入油鍋以中火(約120℃)泡熟撈出, 鍋內留油3大匙燒熱, 隨即入蔥、薑爆香, 再入**2**料及青豆仁, 待滾後放入蝦仁, 並以**3**料勾芡, 灑上麻油淋於鍋粑上即可。

225g.(8oz.)	Shelled shrimp
120g.(4⅓oz.)	Rice cake
50g.(1¾oz.)	Green pea
4 sections	Green onion
3 slices	Ginger
1T.	Sesame oil

1 ½ Egg white
2t.Corn starch
¼t.Salt

2 2C.Stock or water
3T.Tomato ketchup
1T.Sugar
½T.Soy sauce
¼t.Salt

3 2T.each Corn starch, water

❶ Wash and dry shrimp; marinate with **1** for about 20 minutes. Cut rice cake into 3 cm squares (illus. 1).

❷ Heat the wok, add 6C oil; heat to 320°F (160°C). Deep fry rice cake until golden (illus. 2). Place on a large platter.

❸ Soak shrimp in oil (248°F/120°C) until cooked and remove. Keep 3T oil in the wok, heat to hot. Stir fry green onion and ginger until fragant; add in **2** and green pea. When boiled, add in shrimp; thicken with **3** . Sprinkle on sesame oil and pour over rice cake; serve immediately.

❶

❷

沙茶花枝
Fresh Squid with Sha Cha Sauce

花枝 .... 300公克　　洋蔥 100公克
青椒 .... 200公克　　沙茶醬(圖1)...2大匙
油 .... ½小匙

1
- 蛋白　　　1個
- 太白粉　　1大匙

3
- 醬油　　　1大匙
- 蠔油　　　½小匙
- 味精　　　⅛小匙

2
- 紅辣椒片、薑末
- 、蒜末
- 　各1½大匙

4
- 水　　　½大匙
- 太白粉　1小匙

❶ 花枝洗淨切花刀再切成7×4公分之塊狀
　(圖2), 入**1**料醃拌。
❷ 青椒、洋蔥切片備用。
❸ 鍋熱入油3杯燒至七分熱(160℃), 入花枝
　過油(圖3)至熟撈起。
❹ 鍋內留油2大匙, 炒香沙茶醬, 再入**2**料炒
　勻, 隨入青椒、洋蔥拌炒片刻, 再入花枝及
　3料, 起鍋前以**4**料勾芡並淋上麻油。

00g.(10⅔oz.) .... Fresh squid
00g.(7oz.) .... Green pepper
00g.(3½oz.) .... Onion
T. .... Sha Cha sauce (illus 1)
2t. ....Sesame oil

1
- 1 Egg white
- 1T.Corn starch

2
- 1½T.each Red pepper slices,
- 　　　　minced ginger, minced
- 　　　　garlic

3
- 1T.Soy sauce
- ½t.Oyster sauce

4
- ½T.Water
- 1t.Corn starch

❶ Wash squid, cut diagonal slits over the surface and cut into 7 x 4 cm pieces (illus. 2). Marinate in **1** .
❷ Slice green pepper and onion.
❸ Heat the wok, add 3C. oil. Heat to 320°F (160°C), soak squid in hot oil (illus. 3) until done and lift out quickly.
❹ Keep 2T. oil in the wok, stir fry Sha Cha sauce until fragant. Add in **2** and mix evenly. Then add green pepper and onion; fry slightly. Stir in squid and **3** . Thicken with **4** and sprinkle on sesame oil before serving.

薑汁墨魚
Ginger Flavored Fresh Cuttlefish

墨魚...1隻(650公克)　┌淡色醬油、白醋
小黃瓜 .... 3條　　、嫩薑末
鹽 .... ½小匙　**1**　　　　各2大是
　　　　　　　　　麻油　　1大是
　　　　　　　　　糖　　　1小是
　　　　　　　　└鹽　　　½小是

❶ 墨魚洗淨切花刀，再切成6×4公分之斜薄
　片。
❷ 水7杯燒開，將切好的墨魚片入鍋川燙1○
　秒,見肉色轉白時即可撈出,漂涼瀝乾。
❸ 小黃瓜切薄片,加鹽醃10分鐘,再以開水
　洗淨瀝乾、置盤,再將燙好之墨魚片整齊
　舖蓋在上面,最後淋上**1**料即可。
※ 薑汁魚片:將墨魚改成草魚肉(圖1)淨重
　　　　　700公克(不含魚骨),切成薄片
　　　　　(圖2),入鍋川燙時加蔥2段、
　　　　　薑4片(圖3),其他材料及做法
　　　　　與薑汁墨魚同。

650g.(1⅖lb.) ....Fresh cuttlefis
3 ....Small cucumbe
½t. .... Sa
┌2T.each Light brown soy sauce
1　　　　white vinegar, mince
　　　　　　ginger
├1T.Sesame oil
├1t.Sugar
└½t.Salt

❶ Wash cuttlefish, cut diagonal slits over the surface and then cut into 6 x 4 cm
　slanting pieces.
❷ Bring 7C. water to boil, parboil cuttlefish for 10 seconds; lift out as soon as turning
　white. Rinse under cold water and pat dry.
❸ Slice cucumber thinly, marinate with salt for 10 minutes. Rinse with water, dry and
　place on a plate. Arrange cuttlefish neatly over cucumber. Pour **1** over and serve.
※ Ginger Flavored Fish: Use 700g.(1½lb.) of fish fillet (illus. 1) instead of cuttlefish.
　Cut into thin slices (illus. 2). Add 2 green onion sections and ginger slices in the
　water when parboil (illus. 3). The rest of materials and methods remains the same.

❶　❷　❸

紅燒海參
Sea Cucumber with Brown Sauce

海參 450公克
熟筍片 .... ½杯
薑 6片
蔥 6段
香菇 3朵
豆苗 .... ½杯
雞油、麻油.各1大匙

蔥　　　12段
薑　　　 4片

2
高湯　　　　2杯
醬油　　　　2大匙
豬油　　　　1大匙
酒　　　　　1小匙
麻油、糖
　　　　各½小匙
鹽、味精
　　　　各¼小匙

3
水　　　　　2大匙
太白粉　　　1大匙

● 將海參洗淨，斜切成大塊(圖1)。香菇泡軟去蒂(圖2)切斜片。

● 鍋內入水7杯，將**1**料煮開，入海參煮約3分鐘撈起。

● 鍋熱入油3大匙燒熱，炒香蔥、薑，隨入海參及筍片、香菇略炒，再入**2**料燒煮5分鐘，起鍋前入豆苗煮開，並以**3**料勾芡，再淋上雞油及麻油即可。

450g.(1lb.) .... Sea cucumber
½C. .... Boiled bammboo shoot slices
　slices .... Ginger
　sections .... Green onion
　..................... Dried black mushroom
½C. .... Green pea pod tip
T.each .... Chicken fat, sesame oil

[12 sections Green onion
[4 slices Ginger

[2C. Stock
[2T. Soy sauce
[1T. Pork fat
[1t. Cooking wine
[½t. each Sesame oil, sugar
[¼t. Salt

[2T. Water
[1T. Corn starch

❶ Wash sea cucmber and cut into slanting slices (illus. 1). Soften mushroom in hot water, discard the stem (illus. 2) and cut into slanting slices .

❷ Bring 7C. water to boil in a pot with **1**, add in sea cucumber to cook for 3 minutes. Remove and drain.

❸ Heat the wok, add 3T. oil. Stir fry green onion, ginger until fragant. Add in sea cucumber, bamboo, and mushroom, stir fry slightly. Mix in **2** to simmer 5 minutes, add in green pea pod tip. Thicken with **3**. Sprinkle on chicken fat and sesame oil; serve.

家常海參
Sea Cucumber with Hot Sauce

375g.(13⅕oz.)........ Sea cucumber	海參 375公克
250g.(8⅘oz.) .... Bamboo shoot	冬筍 250公克
5 .... Dried black mushroom	香菇 5朵
¾ C. .... Stock	高湯 .... ¾杯
1T.each . White vinegar, chicken fat	白醋、雞油 . 各1大匙
1t. .... Sesame oil	麻油 1小匙

1 — 1T.each Hot soy bean paste, minced ginger, minced green onion
2 — 1½T.Soy sauce / 1T.Sugar
3 — 2T.Water / 1T.Corn starch

1 — 辣豆瓣醬、薑末、蔥末 各1大匙
2 — 醬油 1½大匙 / 糖 1大匙 / 味精 少許
3 — 水 2大匙 / 太白粉 1大匙

❶ 海參洗淨切斜片, 香菇泡軟去蒂與冬筍切3×2公分片狀, 均入開水川燙備用。
❷ 鍋熱入油3大匙, 爆香**1**料, 入高湯、海參、香菇、冬筍與**2**料煮開, 再以**3**料勾芡, 加白醋, 淋上麻油及雞油即可。

❶ Wash sea cucumber and cut into slanting slices. Soften mushroom in hot water and discard the stems. Cut mushroom and bamboo into 3 x 2 cm slices. Parboil.
❷ Heat the wok, add 3T. oil. Stir fry **1** until fragant. Add in stock, sea cucumber, mushroom, bamboo and **2** ; cook until boil. Thickened with **3** , add in white vinegar. Sprinkle on sesame oil and chicken fat. Serve.

瘦肉 225公克	蒜苗 25公克
五香豆干 ... 150公克	紅辣椒絲 10公克

1 — 油 1大匙 / 醬油、太白粉 各¾大匙 / 水 ½大匙
2 — 水 1½大匙 / 醬油、太白粉 各1大匙 / 酒 ½大匙 / 胡椒粉、鹽、麻油 各¼小匙

❶ 豬肉切絲加**1**料拌勻, 蒜苗切斜片、豆干切絲備用。
❷ 鍋熱入油½杯燒至五分熱(120℃)入肉絲翻炒至熟撈出。
❸ 留油2大匙燒熱, 入蒜苗及紅辣椒絲略炒, 再入豆干略炒, 隨即入肉絲及**2**料大火迅速炒拌均勻即可。

香干肉絲
Shredded Pork with Dried Bean Curd

京醬肉絲
Shredded Pork with Peking Sauce

豬肉	300公克		水	2大匙
蔥	145公克		酒	1大匙
甜麵醬	1⅓大匙	**1** 醬油	½大匙
高湯	1大匙		太白粉	2小匙
糖	½小匙		油	1小匙

- 豬肉切成細絲,入**1**料醃約20分鐘;蔥切成細長絲。
- 鍋熱入油3杯燒至五分熱(120℃)入肉絲,肉色變白且散開後,即撈起瀝油。
- 鍋內留油2大匙,入甜麵醬、糖炒香,再入肉絲、高湯同炒,待熟盛起置於蔥絲上即可。

300g.(10⅔oz.)	Pork
145g.(5¹⁄₁₀oz.)	Green onion
1⅓T.	Sweet bean paste
1T.	Stock
½t.	Sugar

1
- 2T.Water
- 1T.Cooking wine
- ½T.Soy sauce
- 2t.Corn starch
- 1t.Oil

- Shred the pork, marinate with **1** for 20 minutes. Shred the green onion.
- Heat the wok, add 3C. oil, and heat to 248°F (120°C). Stir fry pork until whiten and loosen. Lift out and drain.
- Keep 2T. oil in the wok, add in sweet bean paste and sugar. Then add in pork and stock. When cooked, spread over green onion and serve.

25g.(8oz.)	Lean pork
0g.(5⅓oz.)	Dried bean curd
5g.(1oz.)	Fresh garlic leek
0g.(⅓oz.)	Shredded red pepper

1
- 1T.Oil
- ¾T.each Soy sauce, corn starch
- ½T.Water

2
- 1½T.Water
- 1T.each Soy sauce, corn starch
- ½T.Cooking wine
- ¼t.each Pepper, salt, sesame oil

- Shred pork and marinate with **1** . Cut garlic leek into slanting slices; shred dried bean curd.
- Heat the wok, add ½C. oil; heat to 248°F (120°C). Stir fry pork until cooked. Remove pork.
- Keep 2T. oil in the wok, stir fry garlic leek and red pepper; add in bean curd to fry slightly. Continue with pork and **2** ; stir fry over high heat, mix evenly and serve.

榨菜肉絲
Shredded Pork with Pickled Heading Mustard

225g.(8oz.) .... Shredded Pork
65g.(2⅓oz.) .... Yellow chives
50g.(1¾oz.) ....
. Shredded Pickled heading mustard

1
- 1T.each Oil, water
- ¾T.each Soy sauce, corn starch

2
- 1½T.Water
- 1T.Soy sauce
- ½T.Cooking wine
- 1t.Corn starch
- Dash Pepper, sesame oil

豬肉絲.....225公克		韭黃 65公克
榨菜絲.........50公克		

1
- 油、水 各1大匙
- 醬油、太白粉 各¾大匙

2
- 水 1½大匙
- 醬油 1大匙
- 酒 ½大匙
- 太白粉 1小匙
- 胡椒粉、麻油、
- 味精 各少許

❶ 豬肉絲加**1**料拌勻，韭黃洗淨切3公分長段。
❷ 鍋熱入油半杯，入肉絲翻炒至熟撈出。
❸ 留油2大匙，將榨菜絲炒香，再加韭黃略炒，隨入肉絲及**2**料，大火迅速拌炒即可。

❶ Marinate pork with **1** . Wash chive and cut into 3 cm sections.
❷ Heat the wok, add ½C. oil. Stir fry pork until done. Remove.
❸ Keep 2T. oil in the wok, stir fry pickle heading mustard until fragant, stir in chives. Then add in pork and **2** ; stir fry over high heat, mix evenly and serve.

225g.(8oz.) .... Pork fillet
4C. .... Diced toast bread
⅓C..Flour
1 ....Egg

1
- 1t.each Cooking wine, sugar
- ⅓t.Salt
- ⅛t.Pepper

里肌肉........225公克		酒、糖 各1小匙
吐司麵包丁........4杯		鹽 ⅓小匙
麵粉 ....⅓杯		味精 ¼小匙
雞蛋 1個		胡椒粉 ⅛小匙

❶ 里肌肉去除白筋，每隔1公分直切1片，約切成6片，用搥肉器搥鬆，再入**1**料拌勻醃20分鐘。
❷ 將醃好的肉片按麵粉、蛋液、麵包丁等順序兩面沾勻備炸。
❸ 鍋熱入油5杯燒至七分熱(約160℃)，入肉排炸30秒，再翻面炸30秒呈金黃色即可。

❶ Trim off the white sinews on the fillet; cut into 1 cm thick slices, about 6 slices. Loosen with meat beater and marinate in **1** for 20 minutes.
❷ Dip marinated pork in sequence of flour, egg, diced bread. Dip them evenly on both sides.
❸ Heat the wok, add in 5C. oil ; heat to 320°F (160°C). Fry the pork for 3 seconds, then turn the other side for 30 seconds. Lift out and serve when golden.

酥花里肌
Crispy Pork Fillet

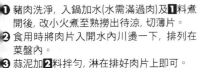

蒜泥白肉
Sliced Pork with Garlic Sauce

後腿肉 450公克	蒜泥 2大匙	
1 蔥 2支 薑 2片 酒 1大匙	**2** 醬油膏 2大匙 紅油、水、細砂 糖 各1大匙 味精 ¼小匙	

450g.(1lb.) .... Pork hind leg
2T. .... Garlic paste
1 2 stalks Green onion 2 slices Ginger 1T.Cooking wine
2 2T.Soy sauce paste 1T.each Chili oil, water, sugar

1 豬肉洗淨，入鍋加水(水需滿過肉)及**1**料煮開後，改小火煮至熟撈出待涼，切薄片。

2 食用時將肉片入開水內川燙一下，排列在菜盤內。

3 蒜泥加**2**料拌勻，淋在排好肉片上即可。

1 Wash the pork; cover with water and boil with **1**. Simmer until cooked. When cooled, slice into thin slices.

2 Before serving, scald pork slices slightly in boiling water. Drain and arrange nicely on a plate.

3 Mix garlic and **2** evenly. Pour over pork and serve.

絞肉 150公克	蔥末 2小匙	
粉絲 70公克	麻油 .... ¼小匙	
1 蔥末 2大匙 辣豆瓣醬 2小匙 薑末 1小匙	**2** 高湯 2杯 醬油 2大匙 糖 1小匙 鹽 ½小匙 味精 ¼小匙	

150g.(5⅓oz.) .... Minced pork
70g.(2½oz.) .... Bean thread
2t. .... Minced green onion
¼t. .... Sesame oil
1 2T.Minced green onion 2t.Hot bean paste 1t.Minced ginger
2 2C.Stock 2T.Soy sauce 1t.Sugar ½t.Salt

1 粉絲泡軟，切長段備用。

2 鍋熱入油4大匙，先入絞肉炒熟，再入**1**料爆香後，放入**2**料及粉絲，改小火燜煮約5分鐘，再灑上蔥末及麻油即可。

1 Soften bean thread in warm water, cut to long sections.

2 Heat the wok, add 4T. oil. Stir fry pork until cooked, then add in **1** until fragant. Continue adding **2** and bean thread; turn the heat to low and simmer for 5 minutes. Sprinkle on minced green onion and sesame oil. Serve.

螞蟻上樹
Ants on the Tree

魚香肉絲
Pork a la Szechwan

里肌肉 .... 300公克　　木耳末 70公克
荸薺 75公克

1
水	2大匙
醬油	1大匙
沙拉油	½大匙
太白粉	2小匙

3
醬油	1大匙
糖	½大匙
酒、麻油、白醋	
太白粉　各1小匙	
水	½小匙
味精	¼小匙

2
| 辣豆瓣醬、蔥末 |
| 、薑末、蒜末 |
| 各1½大匙 |

❶里肌肉去筋(圖1)切成5公分長細絲(圖2
)，拌上**1**料。
❷荸薺用水略煮，撈起漂涼再切碎。
❸鍋熱入油3杯燒五分熱(約120℃)，入肉絲
過油撈起。
❹鍋內留油2大匙將**2**料炒香，續入木耳、荸
薺略炒，隨即入肉絲及**3**料迅速炒拌均勻
即可。
※魚香蝦仁與魚香花枝：將肉絲改爲蝦仁、
　　　　　　花枝，再將**1**料改爲蛋白1個、
　　　　　　太白粉1小匙、鹽⅛小匙，其
　　　　　　他材料及做法與魚香肉絲同。

300g.(10⅔oz.) .... Pork loin
75g.(2⅔oz.) .... Water chestnu‹
70g.(2½oz.) .... Minced wood ear

1
| 2T.Water |
| 1T.Soy sauce |
| ½T.Salad oil |
| 2t.Corn starch |

2
| 1½T.each Hot bean paste, minced |
| ginger, minced green |
| onion, minced garlic |

3
| 1T.Soy sauce |
| ½T.Sugar |
| 1t.each Cooking wine, sesame oil |
| white vinegar, corn starch |
| ½t.Water |

❶ Trim off sinew (illus. 1) and cut pork into 5 cm long thin shreds (illus 2), marinate
with **1** .
❷ Boil water chestnut, lift out and rinse under cold water; minced fine.
❸ Heat the wok, add 3C. oil ; heat to 248°F (120°C). Soak pork in hot oil, and lift
out immediately.
❹ Keep 2T. oil in the wok, stir fry **2** until fragant; add in wood ear and water
chestnut to fry a while. Continue adding in pork and **3** ; stir fry quickly and mix
well. Serve.
※ Shrimp a la Szechwan or Squid a la Szechwan: Replace pork with shrimp or squid.
Replace **1** with 1 egg white, 1t. corn starch, ⅛t. salt. The rest remains the same as
above.

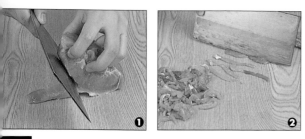

蘭花火腿
Orchid Ham

中式火腿 ...150公克　　火腿末、蔥葉、髮菜
土司 ....6片　　　......................各少許
蛋白 4個

1
冰糖　　200公克
酒釀　　2大匙
蔥　　　1支
薑　　　3片

2
麵粉　　2大匙
太白粉　1大匙

❶ 火腿洗淨切成3公分寬、6公分長的薄片,
上置**1**料蒸1小時備用。

❷ 土司去四週硬邊, 對切成12片長方條, 蛋
白打至起泡, 入**2**料拌勻爲蛋泡。

❸ 每片土司塗上少許蛋泡(圖1),放上火腿片(
圖2),再於火腿上塗一層蛋泡, 並用刀片抹
平(圖3),上面飾以火腿末、蔥葉及髮菜等,
即爲蘭花火腿。

❹ 鍋熱, 入油10杯燒至五分熱(120℃), 將蘭
花火腿入鍋, 炸至金黃色即可。

150g.(5⅓oz.) ....Chinese ham
6 slices ....Toast bread
4 ....Egg white
Dash each ....
Minced ham, green onion, black moss

1
200g.(7oz.)Rock sugar
2T.Sweet fermented rice
1　Green onion
3 slices　Ginger

2
2T.Flour
1T.Corn starch

❶ Wash clean the ham, cut into 3 cm wide, 6 cm long thin slices. Spread **1** over ham and steam for one hour.

❷ Trim off tough edges of the bread, cut to half lengthwise to 12 pieces. Beat egg white to foam, mix in **2** to be egg white paste.

❸ Spread a little egg white paste on each bread (illus. 1), put on ham (illus. 2); and then spread another layer of egg white paste over ham, use a spatula to even the surface (illus. 3). Decorate with minced ham, green onion leaf and black moss to be orchid ham.

❹ Heat the wok, add 10C. oil; heat to 248°F (120°C). Deep fry orchid ham until golden. Serve hot.

糖醋排骨
Sweet and Sour Pork Rib

小排骨 .... 450公克　　蕃茄醬 5大匙
青江菜 5棵

1 ┌ 酒　　　1大匙
　　└ 醬油　　2/3大匙

2 ┌ 蒜、薑末
　　└ 　　　各1大匙

3 ┌ 水　　　3杯
　　│ 糖　　　3大匙
　　│ 白醋　　1⅓大匙
　　│ 酒　　　1大匙
　　│ 醬油　　3/4大匙
　　└ 鹽　　　1/4小匙

4 ┌ 太白粉、水
　　└ 　　　各1小匙

❶ 小排骨切4×2公分塊狀，以**1**料醃20分鐘(圖1)。

❷ 鍋熱入油3杯燒至八分熱(180℃)，入小排炸熟(圖2)，撈起瀝油。

❸ 鍋內留油3大匙，入**2**料爆香，隨入蕃茄醬炒勻，再入**3**料及排骨，以小火燒煮30分鐘至汁收乾，以**4**料勾芡，並以青江菜燙熟盤飾即可。

450g.(1lb.) .... Pork baby rib
5 .... Bok Choy
5T. .... Tomato catchup

1 ┌ 1T.Cooking wine
　　└ 2/3T.Soy sauce

2 ┌ 2T.each Minced garlic, minced
　　└ 　　　　　　　ginger

3 ┌ 3C.Water
　　│ 3T.Sugar
　　│ 1⅓T.White vinegar
　　│ 1T.Cooking wine
　　│ 3/4T.Soy sauce
　　└ 1/4t.Salt

4 1t.each Corn starch, water

❶ Cut ribs into 4 x 2 cm serving pieces, marinate with **1** for 20 minutes (illus. 1).

❷ Heat the wok, add 3C. oil; heat to 356°F (180°C). Fry ribs until cooked (illus. 2), lift out and drain.

❸ Keep 3T. oil in the wok, stir fry **2** until fragant; add in catchup and mix evenly. Then add in **3** and ribs, simmers over low heat for 30 minutes until sauce dried up. Thicken with **4** and serve on a plate decorated with boiled bok choy.

荷葉排骨
Steamed Spare Ribs in Lotus Leaves

豬小排 480公克
荷葉 2張
蒸肉粉 1包
毛豆 18粒

1
沙拉油　　3大匙
水　　　　2大匙
酒釀、醬油、糖
、麻油、辣豆瓣
醬、甜麵醬
　　　　各1大匙
蔥末、薑末
　　　　各1小匙
味精、花椒粉
　　　　各¼小匙

❶ 豬小排剁成10公分長塊狀，加**1**料醃30分
鐘，再拌入蒸肉粉(圖1)。

❷ 荷葉除去硬梗，分成6小張(圖2)，1張荷葉
包1段排骨及3粒毛豆(圖3)，置於碗中，
入蒸籠用大火蒸1個半小時即可。

※ 粉蒸肉：將排骨改成瘦肉300公克，毛豆
改為地瓜120公克，荷葉去掉，所
蒸時間改為40分鐘，其他材料及
做法與荷葉排骨相同。

※ 粉蒸牛肉：將瘦肉改牛肉，所蒸時間為1
小時，其他材料及做法與粉蒸
肉相同。

480g.(1¹⁄₁₀lb.) .... Pork spare rib
2 sheet .... Lotus leaf
1 pack .... Flavored rice powder
18 pcs............................Fresh soy bean

1
3T.Salad oil
2T.Water
1T.each Sweet fermented wine
rice, soy sauce, sugar,
sesame oil, hot soy bean
paste,sweet soy bean
paste
1t.each Minced green onion,
minced ginger
¼t.Szechwan pepper powder

❶ Chop rib into 10 cm long serving pieces, marinate in **1** for 30 minutes; mix in rice powder (illus. 1).

❷ Trim off tough stem and cut each lotus leaf into 6 small pieces (illus. 2). On each lotus leaf, place a rib and 3 fresh soy beans (illus. 3). Put into a steamer and steam over high heat for 1 ½ hours. Serve hot.

※ Steamed Pork with Rice Powder : Replace rib with 300g.(10³⁄₅oz.) lean pork, fresh soy bean with 120g.(4¹⁄₆ oz.) sweet yam. Steam for 40 minutes without lotus leaves. The rest remains the same as above.

※ Steamed Beef with Rice Powder: Replace lean pork with beef. Steam for one hour. The rest remains the same as steamed pork.

木須肉
Mu-Shu Pork

里肌肉 150公克		鹽 .... 少許
蛋 2個		

1
- 水　　　1½大匙
- 醬油、油
- 　　　　各2小匙
- 太白粉　1小匙

2
- 熟筍絲 150公克
- 韭黃　 75公克
- 濕木耳絲35公克

3
- 醬油　　1大匙
- 酒　　　1小匙
- 鹽　　　½小匙
- 味精　　¼小匙

❶ 里肌肉切絲入**1**料拌勻醃10分鐘。
❷ 韭黃切4公分長段(圖1)，蛋加少許鹽打散備用。
❸ 鍋熱入油4大匙，入肉絲炒熟撈出。蛋液炒至剛熟(圖2)，隨加入**2**、**3**料及肉絲，以大火拌炒約1分鐘即可。
※ 此菜可用荷葉餅或木須皮沾海鮮醬包食。

150g.(5⅓oz.) .... Pork loin	
2 .... Egg	
Dash .... Salt	

1
- 1½T. Water
- 2t. each Soy sauce, oil
- 1t. Corn starch

2
- 150g.(5⅓oz.) Cooked shrdded bamboo shoot
- 75g.(2⅔oz.) Yellow chive
- 35g.(1⅓oz.) Shrdded wood ear

3
- 1T. Soy sauce
- 1t. Cooking wine
- ½t. Salt

❶ Shred pork and marinate with **1** for 10 minutes.
❷ Cut yellow chives into 4 cm long sections (illus. 1). Beat egg with a dash of salt.
❸ Heat the wok, add 4T. oil; stir fry pork until cooked, lift out. Fry egg to soft form (illus. 2), add in **2** , **3** , and pork; stir fry over high heat for about one minute. Remove and serve.
※ Can be served with mu-shu skins and Hoi Sin Sauce.

回鍋肉
Twice Cooked Pork

豬後腿肉 ...300公克
青椒 1個
蒜苗 1支
薑 2片

1
┌ 辣豆瓣醬 1大匙
│ 醬油、甜麵醬、
│ 酒 各½大匙
└ 糖 1小匙

❶ 豬肉洗淨，入鍋加水(圖1)煮開後，改小火煮約30分鐘取出，待冷切薄片(圖2)。
❷ 青椒洗淨去籽切三角塊，蒜苗切斜段，將蒜白及蒜葉分開。
❸ 鍋熱入油2大匙，先爆炒肉片，再下蒜白、青椒同炒盛起。
❹ 另油2大匙燒熱，入薑片再入**1**料炒香，隨即入豬肉、青椒、蒜白拌炒，起鍋前再加入蒜葉拌勻即可。

300g.(10⅔oz.) ....Pork hind leg
1 .... Green pepper
1 .... Garlic leek
2 slices .... Ginger

1
┌ 1T.Hot soy bean paste
│ ½T.each Soy sauce, sweet soy
│ bean paste, cooking
│ wine
└ 1t.Sugar

❶ Wash pork, put in a pot and add water (illus. 1). When boil, turn down heat to simmer for 30 minutes; lift out and drain. Slice thin when cooled (illus. 2).
❷ Cut green pepper to triangular pieces; garlic leek to slanting sections, separating white and green parts.
❸ Heat the wok, add 2T. oil; stir fry pork first, add in garlic leek white parts and green pepper to fry. Remove.
❹ Heat 2T. oil to hot, stir fry ginger, add in **1** ; fry until fragant. Then add in pork, pepper, garlic whites; mix evenly. Before removing from the wok, mix in garlic leek green parts. Serve.

蔥串斑脂
Intestine Rings on Green Onion Fingers

大腸頭	2條	花椒鹽	少許
蔥	6支		

1
- 蔥 1支
- 薑 1片
- 酒 2大匙

2
- 醬油 2大匙
- 鹽 ..... ¼小匙

❶ 大腸去油脂(圖1)洗淨，入鍋川燙後再洗淨，加**1**料入鍋煮至筷子能插入。

❷ 取出大腸，趁熱將蔥穿入大腸中(圖2)，再入**2**料略醃。

❸ 鍋熱入油3杯燒至八分熱(180℃)，入大腸以大火炸至金黃色撈出，切斜片，食時沾花椒鹽即可。

2 pieces	Pig intestine (head part)
6	Green onion
Dash	Szechwan pepper salt

1
- 1 Green onion
- 1 slice Ginger
- 2T. Cooking wine

2
- 2T. Soy sauce
- ¼t. Salt

❶ Trim off fat (illus. 1) and wash intestine. Scald in boiling water and then wash again. Boil in water with **1** until chop stick can easily pierce through.

❷ Lift out intestine, stuff green onion into center while still warm (illus. 2). Marinate in **2** .

❸ Heat the wok, add 3C. oil; heat to 356°F (180°C). Deep fry intestine until golden. Cut into slanting slices and serve. Dip in Szechwan pepper salt when eating.

五更腸旺
Pig Intestine in Fire Pot

大腸頭	2條	蒜苗		1支
雞血	1塊			

1
- 蔥 1支
- 薑 1片
- 酒 2大匙

3
- 高湯 1杯
- 醬油 2大匙
- 酒 1大匙
- 味精 .... ¼小匙

2
- 辣豆瓣醬 1½大匙
- 蒜末、薑末 .. 各1大匙
- 花椒粒 ...... ¼小匙

4
- 太白粉、水 .. 各1大匙
- 麻油 1小匙

❶ 大腸頭洗淨入鍋川燙(圖1)再洗淨，加**1**料入鍋煮至熟透，切菱形(圖2)。

❷ 雞血切菱形(圖3)，再以熱水川燙。蒜苗切斜片備用。

❸ 鍋熱入油3大匙燒熱，爆香**2**料，再入**3**料、大腸頭、雞血改小火煮開後，續煮4—5分鐘，再以**4**料勾芡並入蒜苗拌勻即可。

2 pieces	Pig intestine
1 piece	Chicken blood
1	Garlic leek

1
- 1 Green onion
- 1 slice Ginger
- 2T. Cooking wine

2
- 1½T. Hot soy bean paste
- 1T. each Minced garlic, minced ginger
- ¼t. Szechwan pepper corn

3
- 1C. Stock
- 2T. Soy sauce
- 1T. Cooking wine

4
- 1T. each Corn starch, water
- 1t. Sesame oil

❶ Wash intestine; scald in boiling water (illus. 1) and then wash again. Boil in water with **1** until tender; cut into diamond shaped serving pieces (illus. 2).

❷ Cut chicken blood into diamond shaped serving pieces (illus. 3); parboil in boiling water. Cut garlic leek into slanting slices.

❸ Heat the wok, add 3T. oil; heat to hot, stir fry **2** until fragant. Add in **3**, intestine, and chicken blood; turn down heat to low. Continue cooking another 4 to 5 minutes after boiling. Thicken with **4** and mix in garlic leek evenly. Serve hot.

紅燒牛腩
Beef Stew

牛腩 370公克	青江菜 4棵

1 蔥　　　　1支
　　薑　　　　1片
　　辣豆瓣醬　1大匙
　　花椒粒　　1小匙

2 水　　　　7杯
　　醬油　　　2大匙
　　糖色　　　1大匙
　　糖　　　　1小匙

3 水　　　　1大匙
　　太白粉、麻油
　　　　　　各1小匙

❶ 鍋熱入油1大匙炒香**1**料備用，牛腩川燙洗淨，入已炒香之**1**料及**2**料，煮開後改小火煮1小時，撈出瀝乾，待冷後切6公分長條(圖1)，原汁去渣備用(圖2)。

❷ 將牛腩排入湯碗內(圖3)，倒入原汁同蒸1小時，至牛腩熟爛。

❸ 倒出牛腩汁，牛腩倒扣盤中，燉汁加入**3**料勾芡後，淋在牛腩上。青江菜洗淨後整棵燙熟，排在盤邊點綴。

370g.(13oz.) .... Beef brisket	
4 .... Bok Choy	

1 1½T. Hot soy bean paste
　 1t. Szechwan pepper corn
　 1 Green onion
　 1 slice Ginger

2 7C. Water
　 2T. Soy sauce
　 1T. Sugar coloring
　 1t. Sugar

3 1T. Water
　 1t. each Corn starch, sesame oil

❶ Heat the wok, add 1T. oil; stir fry **1** until fragant.

❷ Parboil beef and wash clean. Simmer in **2** with fried **1** for one hour after boiling. Lift out and cool, cut into 6 cm long stirps (illus. 1). Sieve the juice clear for later use (illus. 2).

❸ Arrange beef in a soup bowl (illus. 3), pour over the juice and steam for one hour until beef is very tender. Pour off the juice.

❹ Wash and boil bok choy; drain and arrange around the edge of a plate.

❺ Turn beef upside down onto the center of plate. Thicken juice with **3** and pour over beef. Serve.

鐵板牛排
Beef Steak on Sizzling Plate

牛排肉 .... 300公克 　紅辣椒 2條
洋蔥 .... 220公克 　太白粉 3大匙

1
蔥　　　　8段
薑　　　　4片
醬油、酒
　　　各1大匙
小蘇打、胡椒粉
　　　各¼小匙

2
蕃茄醬、水
　　　各2大匙
醬油、黑醋
　　　各1小匙
糖、胡椒粉
　　　各½小匙
味精　　¼小匙

- 牛肉洗淨切片, 用肉槌或刀背拍鬆(圖1), 再加**1**料醃20分鐘, 使之入味後, 沾太白粉(圖2)備用。
- 洋蔥切絲, 紅辣椒去籽切斜片, 鐵板燒熱備用。
- 鍋熱入油3杯燒至六分熱(140℃), 將紅辣椒、洋蔥過油, 隨即撈起, 瀝油盛於鐵盤上。
- 鍋內留油3大匙, 將醃過牛排入鍋兩面煎黃(圖3), 再入**2**料拌勻置於洋蔥上即可。

00g.(10⅔oz.) ....Beef steak meat
20g.(7⅘ oz.) .... Onion
.... Hot red pepper

1
8 sections　Green onion
4 slices　Ginger
1T.each Soy sauce, cooking wine
¼t.each Sugar, pepper

2
2T.each Tomato catchup, water
1t.each Soy sauce, black vinegar
½t.each Sugar, pepper

① Wash beef and slice; loosen beef with a meat beater or the back of knife (illus. 1), marinate in **1** for 20 minutes. Then dip in corn starch (illus. 2).

② Shred onion; discard seeds in red pepper and cut into slanting slices. Preheat the sizzling plate.

③ Heat the wok, add 3C. oil; heat to 284°F (140°C). Soak onion and red pepper in hot oil and lift out immediately; drain and place on hot plate.

④ Keep 3T.oil in the wok, fry marinated beef to golden on both sides (illus. 3); mix in **2** evenly. Place beef over onion and serve.

家常牛肉絲
Shredded Beef Home Style

牛肉 ....300公克　薑絲、辣椒絲、辣豆
芹菜 ....100公克　瓣醬(圖1)..各1大匙
蒜苗 50公克

1　油　　　2大匙　　**3**　水　　　1大匙
　　　醬油　　　2小匙　　　　太白粉　　1小匙
　　　小蘇打　　⅛小匙
2　醬油　　　1小匙　　**4**　酒　　　½大匙
　　　味精　　　¼小匙　　　　麻油、白醋
　　　　　　　　　　　　　　　　　各1小匙

❶ 牛肉洗淨, 切絲, 入**1**料醃10分鐘。
❷ 芹菜洗淨, 去頭、葉, 切3公分分段(圖2)
　 蒜苗切斜片。
❸ 鍋熱入油3杯燒至五分熱(120℃)放入牛
　 肉,見肉色變白即撈起瀝油, 再入芹菜、蒜
　 苗過油, 隨即取出瀝油, 備用。
❹ 鍋中留油1大匙, 入薑絲、辣椒絲爆香後
　 入辣豆瓣醬炒勻, 再加入牛肉、芹菜、蒜
　 苗及**2**料翻炒均勻, 以**3**料勾芡, 起鍋時淋
　 下**4**料即可。

300g.(10⅔oz.)............................Beef
100g.(3½oz.) .... Celery
50g.(2¾oz.) ....Fresh garlic leek
1T.each............ Shredded red pepper,
hot bean paste, shredded ginger (illus. 1)

1　┌ 2T.Oil
　　　│ 2t.Soy sauce
　　　└ ⅛t.Baking soda
2　1t.Soy sauce
3　┌ 1T.Water
　　　└ 1t.Corn starch
4　┌ ½T.Cooking wine
　　　└ 1t.each White vinegar, sesame oil

❶ Wash and shred beef; marinate in **1** for 10 minutes.
❷ Wash celery, discard root and leave ; cut into 3 cm sections(illus. 2). Cut garlic leek into slanting slices.
❸ Heat the wok, add 3C. oil; heat to 248°F (120°C). Soak beef in hot oil until color turns pale; remove and drain. Then soak celery and garlic leek in hot oil, lift out immediately.
❹ Keep 1T. oil in the wok, add in ginger, red pepper; stir fry until fragant. Then mix in bean paste, continue adding beef, celery, garlic leek and **2** ; stir fry and mix well. Thicken with **3** ; sprinkle on **4** and serve.

❶　❷

干扁牛肉絲
Spicy Dry Fried Beef

牛肉 .... 300公克　　芹菜 70公克
\ 蘿蔔 ...... 100公克　　蒜苗 1支
辣豆瓣醬 .... 1大匙　　花椒粉 ...... ⅓小匙

1
┌ 蔥　　　　　5段
├ 薑絲、紅辣椒絲
│　　　　　各1大匙

2
┌ 酒　　　　　1大匙
├ 醬油　　　　½大匙
├ 糖　　　　　2小匙
└ 味精　　　　¼小匙

3
┌ 麻油　　　　1小匙
└ 白醋　　　　½小匙

● 將牛肉切成0.5×5公分條狀, 紅蘿蔔、蒜
苗切0.4×3公分之條狀, 芹菜切3公分段
備用。

● 油3杯燒至七分熱(160℃), 入牛肉絲炸至
乾硬, 撈起瀝油備用, 另入紅蘿蔔絲、蒜苗
絲、芹菜段於油鍋中過油, 隨即撈起瀝油
備用。

● 鍋內留油1大匙, 先爆香**1**料, 再入辣豆瓣
醬炒香, 隨入牛肉絲、紅蘿蔔絲、蒜苗、
芹菜及**2**料拌炒均勻, 起鍋前淋上**3**料炒
勻,盛在菜盤上, 上面再撒花椒粉即可。

00g.(10⅔oz.)	Beef
00g.(3½oz.)	Carrot
0g.(2½oz.)	Celery
T.	Hot bean paste
3t.	Szechwan pepper powder
	Garlic leek

1
┌ 5 sections Green onion
├ 1T.each Shredded ginger,
│　　　　　shredded red pepper

2
┌ 1T.Cooking wine
├ ½T.Soy sauce
└ 2t.Sugar

3
┌ 1t.Sesame oil
└ ½t.Vinegar

❶ Cut beef into 0.5 x 5 cm long strips; carrot and garlic leek into 0.4 x 3 cm long strips. Cut celery into 3 cm long sections.

❷ Heat the wok, add 3C. oil; heat to 320°F (160°C). Fry beef strips until dry and hard, lift out and drain. Soak carrot, garlic leek and celery in hot oil; lift out immediately.

❸ Keep 1T. oil in the wok, stir fry **1** until fragrant; add in hot bean paste to fry. Then add in beef, carrot, garlic,celery and **2** ; stir fry and mix well. Mix in **3** evenly. Remove to a plate; sprinkle on Szechwan pepper powder and serve.

青椒牛肉片
Beef with Green Pepper

牛肉...........300公克	紅辣椒...............2條
青椒...........150公克	薑....................2片
蔥....................4段	蒜片...............1大匙

1
- 水　　　　1大匙
- 醬油、沙拉油
　　　　　各½大匙
- 太白粉　　1小匙
- 小蘇打　　¼小匙

2
- 水　　　　1大匙
- 蠔油、酒
　　　　　各½大匙
- 醬油、麻油、太白粉　各1小匙
- 糖　　　　⅓小匙
- 味精、胡椒粉
　　　　　各¼小匙

❶ 牛肉切薄片入**1**料醃10分鐘，青椒、紅辣椒切片備用。

❷ 鍋熱入油3杯燒至五分熱(120℃)，入牛肉見肉色變白即撈起瀝油，再入青椒過油，隨即撈起瀝油備用。

❸ 鍋內留油1大匙，將蔥段、紅辣椒片、薑片、蒜片爆香，再入牛肉、青椒拌炒，並加**2**料，炒拌均勻即可。

300g.(10⅔oz.)............................Beef
150g.(5⅓oz.) ....Green pepper
2 slices.....................................Ginger
2 ....Red pepper
4 sections........................ Green onion
1T. ....Sliced garlic

1
- 1T.Water
- ½T.each Soy sauce, salad oil
- 1t.Corn starch
- ¼t.Baking soda

2
- 1T.Water
- ½T.each Oyster sauce, cooking wine
- 1t.each Soy sauce, sesame oil, corn starch
- ⅓t.Sugar
- ¼t.Pepper

❶ Slice beef thin and marinate in **1** for 10 minutes. Slice red pepper and green pepper.

❷ Heat the wok, add 3C. oil; heat to 248°F (120°C). Soak beef in hot oil until beef turns pale, lift out and drain. Soak green pepper in hot oil, immediately lift out and drain.

❸ Keep 1T. oil in the wok, stir fry green onion, red pepper, ginger, and garlic until fragant. Add in beef and green pepper to fry; then add in **2** . Mix evenly and serve.

雀巢牛柳
Sliced Beef in Potato Nest

牛肉片 .... 300公克 　　蔥 8段

馬鈴薯 .... 220公克 　　廣東生菜、薑 .各4片

1
- 油、水　各1大匙
- 醬油　　½大匙
- 太白粉　1小匙
- 小蘇打　¼小匙

2
- 太白粉　1小匙
- 鹽　　　¼小匙

3
- 青椒片　100公克
- 洋蔥片　60公克
- 紅辣椒　20公克

4
- 醬油、酒　各½大匙
- 麻油、水　各1小匙
- 太白粉、胡椒粉、味精　各½小匙

❶ 牛肉片加**1**料拌勻醃30分鐘。

❷ 馬鈴薯去皮刨成細絲，入**2**料拌勻，油6杯燒至七分熱(160℃)，將馬鈴薯放入漏杓內，入鍋炸成型，即為雀巢。

❸ 油再燒至六分熱(140℃)，入牛肉片，再入**3**料拌勻，隨即一同撈起。留油1大匙爆香蔥、薑，續入牛肉片、**3**料與**4**料拌炒均勻盛於雀巢內即可。

※ 雀巢蝦仁：將雀巢牛柳之牛肉改為蝦仁，**1**料改為蛋白1個、太白粉1大匙，其餘材料及做法均與雀巢牛柳同。

300g.(10⅔oz.) .... Sliced beef

220g.(7¾oz.) .... Potato

3 sections .... Green onion

4 slices .... Ginger

4 pieces .... Roman lettuce

1
- 1T.each Oil, water
- ½T.Soy sauce
- 1t.Corn starch
- ¼t.Baking soda

2
- 1t.Corn starch
- ¼t.Salt

3
- 100g.(3½oz.)Sliced green pepper
- 60g.(2¹⁄₁₀oz.)Sliced onion
- 20g.(⁵⁄₇oz.)Sliced red pepper

4
- ½T.each Soy sauce, cooking wine
- 1t.each Sesame oil, water
- ½t.each Corn starch,pepper

❶ Marinate sliced beef in **1** for 30 minutes.

❷ Shave potato into fine threads, mix evenly with **2** . Heat the wok, add 6C. oil; heat to 320°F (160°C). Place potato in a metal sieve, low into oil and fry to bird's nest form. Remove.

❸ Heat oil to 284°F (140°C), soak beef first, then add in **3** to mix evevly; lift out together immediately. Keep 1T. oil in the wok, stir fry green onion and ginger until fragant. Add in beef, **3** , and **4** ; stir fry evenly. Place into nest and serve.

※ Shrimp in Potato Nest: Substitute beef with shrimp. Change **1** to 1 egg white and 1T. corn starch. The rest remains the same.

麻辣牛筋
Spicy Beef Tendon

300g.(10⅔oz.)	Beef tendon
3	Green onion
1 slice	Ginger
1T.	Cooking wine

1 ⌈ 1T.Stock
  │ 2t.Chili oil
  │ 1t.each White vinegar, sugar
  │ ½t.each Salt, Szechwan
  └   pepper powder

牛筋	300公克
蔥	3支
薑	1片
酒	1大匙

1 ⌈ 高湯   1大匙
  │ 紅油   2小匙
  │ 白醋、砂糖、味
  │ 精   各1小匙
  │ 鹽、花椒粉
  └   各½小匙

❶ 牛筋加蔥1支、薑、酒煮至爛(約5小時)，餘蔥切斜段備用。
❷ 將牛筋切薄片，加蔥段與**1**料拌勻即可食用。

❶ Braise beef tendon with 1 green onion, ginger and wine until tender (approx. 5 hours). Cut remaining 2 green onions into slanting sections.
❷ Cut beef tendon into thin slices. Mix with green onion and **1** ; serve.

牛肉	300公克		酒釀	½大匙
高湯	½杯		鹽	½小匙

1 ⌈ 乾辣椒   ½杯
  │ 陳皮   1大匙
  │ 花椒粒   ½大匙
  └ 八角   1小匙

2 ⌈ 糖   1大匙
  │ 酒   ½大匙
  │ 鹽   ½小匙
  └ 味精   ¼小匙

3 ⌈ 白醋   1小匙
  └ 麻油   ½小匙

❶ 牛肉切成 4×1.5×0.3公分片狀，加鹽醃20分。
❷ 油3杯燒至七分熱(160℃)，牛肉入鍋炸至六分熟(約30秒)撈起瀝油。
❸ 鍋中留油2大匙，入**1**料爆香，再入肉片、高湯、酒釀及**2**料一起燒，待湯汁快收乾時，加**3**料拌勻即可。

陳皮牛肉
Beef with Orange Flavor

涼拌牛筋
Cold Beef Shank

牛筋 .... 300公克　　蔥白 3支
香菜(切段) ... 15公克

1
水　　　1大鍋
蔥　　　1支
薑　　　1片
酒　　　1大匙

2
醬油　　　2大匙
蒜末、糖、麻
油　　各1大匙
白醋　　　½大匙

300g.(10⅔oz.)..............Beef shank
15g.(½oz.) ....Coriander sections
3 ....Green onion (white part only)

1
1 large pot Water
1　Green onion
1 slice　Ginger
1 T.Cooking wine

2
2 T.Soy sauce
1 T.each　Minced garlic, sugar,
　　　　　sesame oil
½ T.White vinegar

1 將牛筋洗淨，與**1**料用小火煮5小時後，撈
起放涼，再切薄片，蔥白切斜段備用。
2 香菜平舖在盤子中央，把牛筋片與蔥白擺
於其上，將**2**料拌勻後淋於其上即可。

1 Wash beef and simmer with **1** for 5 hours. Drain and cool; cut into thin slices.
Cut green onions into slanting sections.
2 Spread parsley at the center of a plate. Arrange beef slices and green onion
sections over coriander. Pour over **2** and serve.

300g.(10⅔oz.) ....Beef
½C. .... Stock
½T. ....Fermented wine rice
½t. ....Salt

1
½C.Dried red pepper
1 T.Dried orange peel
½T.Szechwan pepper corn
1 t.Star anise

2
1 T.Sugar
½T.Cooking wine
½t.Salt

3
1 t.White vinegar
½t.Sesame oil

1 Cut beef into 4 x 1.5 x 0.3 cm slices, marinate with salt for 20 minutes.
2 Heat the wok, add 3C. oil; heat to 320°F (160°C). Fry beef to medium cooked
(approx. 30 seconds), lift out and drain.
3 Keep 2T. oil in the wok, stir fry **1** until fragant. Add in beef, stock, wine rice
and **2** to cook together. When sauce nearly dried out, mix in **3** evenly and
serve.

宮保雞丁
Spicy Kun-Pao Chicken

雞胸肉 .... 300公克　　蒜頭花生 .... ½杯

1	乾辣椒　　¾杯
	花椒粒　　1小匙
2	蔥　　　　6段
	薑末　　　1小匙
3	醬油、水　各1大匙
	太白粉　　2小匙

4	水　　　　　2大匙
	糖色、酒、白醋、醬油　各1大匙
	麻油　　　　½大匙
	糖　　　　　2小匙
	太白粉　　　½小匙
	味精　　　　¼小匙

❶ 乾辣椒切段，去籽備用。

❷ 雞肉略拍鬆(圖1)後切成1.5x1.5公分之丁狀(圖2)，入**3**料拌醃10分鐘。鍋熱入油4杯，燒至六分熱(約140℃)，入雞丁過油後(圖3)，撈起備用。

❸ 鍋內留油3大匙，入**1**料炒香，再入**2**料爆香後，續入雞丁與**4**料，以大火炒拌均勻起鍋前加入蒜頭花生拌勻即可。

※ 炒香乾辣椒時，油溫不可太高，以免將乾辣椒炒得太黑。

※ 宮保魷魚：將雞丁改為魷魚450公克。魷魚不需以**3**料醃，**4**料中再加入鹽½小匙、太白粉½大匙其餘材料及做法與宮保雞丁同。

300g.(10⅔oz.)............Chicken breast
½C................................Garlic peanut

1	¾C.Dried red pepper (kun-pao)
	1t.Szechwan pepper corn
2	6 sections　Green onion
	1t.Minced ginger
3	1T.each Soy sauce, water
	2t.Corn starch
4	2T.water
	1T.each Sugar coloring, cooking wine, white vinegar, soy sauce
	½T.Sesame oil
	2t.Sugar
	½t.Corn starch

❶ Cut red pepper into sections, discard seeds.

❷ Loosen chicken breast (illus. 1) and cut into 1.5 x 1.5 cm cubes (illus. 2); marinate with **3** for 10 minutes. Heat the wok, add 4C. oil, heat to 284°F (140°C). Soak chicken in hot oil (illus. 3); lift out immediately and drain.

❸ Keep 3T. oil in the wok, stir fry **1** until fragant; add in **2** to fry. Then add in chicken and **4** ; stir fry over high heat until evenly mixed. Mix in garlic peanut before removing.

※ Oil should not be too hot when frying red pepper, to avoid red pepper turning black.

※ Kun-Pao Cuttlefish: Substitute chicken with 450g.(1lb.) squid. Squid does not need to marinate in **3** . Add ½t. salt and ½T. corn starch additionally into **4** . The rest remains the same as above.

雀巢雞丁
Diced Chicken in Taro Nest

雞腿肉 ...... 300公克　　廣東生菜 4片
芋頭 .... 225公克　　薑 2片
蔥 8段

1
醬油、水
　　　　各1大匙
太白粉　　2小匙
酒　　　　1小匙

2
太白粉　　1小匙
鹽　　　　¼小匙

3
青椒丁　100公克
洋蔥丁　　60公克
紅辣椒　　20公克

4
醬油、酒
　　　　各½大匙
麻油、水
　　　　各1小匙
太白粉　　½小匙
胡椒粉、味精
　　　　各¼小匙

❶ 雞腿洗淨去骨, 切成2×2公分方塊, 以**1**料
　拌勻醃30分鐘。
❷ 芋頭去皮刨成細絲(圖1), 入**2**料拌勻(圖2
　)。油6杯燒至七分熱(約160℃), 將芋絲放
　入漏杓內(圖3), 入鍋炸成型, 即爲雀巢。
　盤內鋪放生菜葉, 雀巢置於其上備用。
❸ 油再燒至六分熱(約140℃), 入雞丁, 再入
　3料拌勻, 隨即一同撈起。留油1大匙爆
　香蔥、薑, 續入雞丁、**3**料與**4**料拌炒均
　勻, 盛於雀巢內即可。

300g.(10⅔oz.) .... Chicken leg
225g.(8oz.) .... Taro
8 sections .... Green onion
4 leaves .... Roman lettuce
2 slices .... Ginger

1
1T.each Soy sauce, water
2t.Corn starch
1t.Cooking wine

2
1t.Corn starch
¼t.Salt

3
100g.(3½oz.) Diced green pepper
60g.(2oz.) Diced onion
20g.(⅔oz.) Diced red pepper

4
½T.each Soy sauce, cooking wine
1t.each Sesame oil, water
½t.Corn starch
¼t.Pepper

❶ Clean chicken leg and discard the bone; cut into 2 cm cubes, and marinate with **1** for 30 minutes.
❷ Peel off taro skin and shredded to thin shreds (illus. 1), mix with **2** well (illus. 2). Heat the wok, add 6C. oil; heat to 320°F (160°C). Place taro shreds in a sieve (illus. 3). Deep fry to form a taro nest.
❸ Reheat oil to 284°F (140°C); soak chicken in hot oil, then mix in **3** ; immediately lift out all together. Keep 1T. oil in the wok, stir fry green onion and ginger until fragant. Then add in chicken, **3** , and **4** ; stir fry and mix well. Place into the taro nest and serve.

腰果雞丁
Diced Chicken with Cashew Nuts

雞肉 .... 300公克　　青椒 100公克
炸熟腰果 ... 100公克

1┌ 水　　　　　1大匙
　├ 醬油、太白粉
　└　　　　　各½大匙

3┌ 水、醬油
　│　　　　　各1大匙
　│ 酒、太白粉
　│　　　　　各½大匙
　│ 麻油　　　1小匙
　└ 胡椒粉　　⅛小匙

2┌ 蔥　　　　　5段
　└ 薑　　　　　6片

❶ 雞肉切成1.5×1.5公分之小丁，入**1**料拌醃30分鐘。青椒去籽亦切小丁備用。

❷ 油2杯燒至五分熟(約120℃)，入雞丁過油後撈出，留油1大匙，入**2**料爆香，再入青椒快炒，最後入雞丁與**3**料拌炒，起鍋前加入腰果即可。

※ 腰果蝦仁：將腰果雞丁之雞丁改為蝦仁，青椒改為毛豆2大匙，**1**料改為蛋白1個、太白粉1大匙、鹽⅛小匙，其餘材料及做法均與腰果雞丁同。

300g.(10⅔oz.) .... Chicken meat
100g.(3½oz.) .... Fried cashew nut
100g.(3½oz.) .... Green pepper

1┌ 1T.Water
　└ ½T.each Soy sauce, corn starch

2┌ 5 sections　Green onion
　└ 6 slices　Ginger

3┌ 1T.each Water, soy sauce
　│ ½T.each Cooking wine, corn
　│　　　　　　starch
　│ 1t.Sesame oil
　└ ⅛t.Pepper

❶ Cut chicken into 1.5 x 1.5 cm dices, marinate with **1** for 30 minutes. Discard the seeds and dice green pepper.

❷ Heat the wok, add 2C. oil; heat to 248°F (120°C). Soak chicken in hot oil and lift out to drain. Keep 1T. oil in the wok, stir fry **2** until fragant, then add in green pepper to fry. Finally add in chicken and **3** to stir fry and mix well. Add in cashew nuts before serving.

※ Shrimp with cashew nuts: Replace chicken with shrimp, green pepper with 2T. fresh soy bean; **1** with 1 egg white, 1T. corn starch and ⅛t. salt. The rest remains the same as above.

芙蓉雞片
Chicken Fu-Yun

雞柳...150公克(2條)　　蛋白..................3個
洋菇片.........75公克　　中式火腿片..75公克
蔥......................8段　　豌豆莢.........40公克
薑......................4片　　香菇..................2朵
雞油...............2大匙

1
水　　　　3大匙
太白粉　　½大匙
味精、鹽、酒
　　　各¼小匙
胡椒粉　　⅛小匙

2
高湯　　　1杯
鹽　　　　½小匙
味精　　　⅛小匙

3
水　　　　1大匙
太白粉　　1小匙

1 雞肉去筋(圖1)，打成泥狀(圖2)，加**1**料拌勻，蛋白打發加入，拌成肉泥糊。香菇泡軟去蒂切片備用。

2 鍋熱入油5杯燒至四分熱(100℃)，用湯匙將肉泥鏟成一片片(圖3)入鍋，炸至熟即撈起瀝油。

3 水6杯燒開，入雞片煮片刻以去油脂，豌豆莢去硬莖、洋菇入鍋川燙備用。

4 油2大匙燒熱，入蔥、薑爆香，續入**2**料煮開後，撈起蔥、薑，再入火腿、雞肉、豌豆莢、洋菇及香菇炒熟，以**3**料勾芡，淋上雞油即可。

150g.(5⅓oz.) ....Chicken breast
75g.(2⅔oz.)...............Sliced mushroom
75g.(2⅔oz.).........Sliced Chinese ham
40g.(1⅖oz.) ....Snow pea pod
3...Egg white
8 sections ....Green onion
4 slices....................................Ginger
2........................Dried black mushroom
2T. ....Chicken fat

1
3T.Water
½T.Corn starch
¼t.each Salt, cooking wine
⅛t.Pepper

2
1C.Stock
½t.Salt

3
1T.Water
1t.Corn starch

1 Trim off sinew (illus. 1), beat it to mash (illus. 2); mix well with **1** . Beat egg white and add into chicken mash. Soften black mushroom with warm water; discard stems and slice.

2 Heat the wok, add 5C. oil; heat to 212°F (100°C). With a spoon to form chicken mash to slices (illus. 3); fry in hot oil until cooked. Lift out and drain.

3 Bring 6C. water to boil, add in chicken pieces for a moment to rid of excessive grease. Peel off tough fiber of snow pea pod; scald mushroom in boiling water.

4 Heat 2T. oil, stir fry green onion and ginger to fragant; add in **2** to boil, discard green onion and ginger. Then add in ham, chicken, snow pea pod, mushroom and black mushroom to stir fry. Thicken with **3** , sprinkle on chicken fat and serve.

300g.(10⅔oz.) .... Chicken breast
1T. .... Minced lemon peel

1
- 1 Egg yolk
- 1T. Corn starch
- 1½t. Soy sauce
- 1t. Cooking wine
- ¼t. Salt
- ⅛t. Pepper

2
- 4T. Corn starch
- 2T. Flour

3
- 3T. Water
- 2T. each Lemon juice, sugar
- ½t. Corn starch
- ¼t. Salt

雞胸肉 300公克	檸檬皮末 1大匙
1 太白粉　1大匙 蛋黃　1個 醬油　1½小匙 酒　1小匙 鹽　¼小匙 胡椒粉　⅛小匙	**2** 太白粉　4大匙 麵粉　2大匙 水　3大匙 **3** 檸檬汁、糖 　各2大匙 太白粉　½小匙 鹽　¼小匙

❶ 雞胸肉去皮，切成 3×2 公分之大薄片，入 **1** 料醃10分鐘，炸前再沾預先拌勻之 **2** 料。

❷ 鍋熱入油 3 杯，燒至八分熱(180℃)，入雞片，炸熟撈出，油再燒熱，雞片回炸10秒盛盤。

❸ 鍋內留油 1 大匙，將 **3** 料煮開，淋在雞片上，再撒上檸檬皮末即可。

❶ Skin chicken breast; cut into 3 x 2 cm large thin slices. Marinate in **1** for 10 minutes. Dip in evenly mixed **2** before frying.

❷ Heat the wok, add 3C. oil; heat to 356°F (180°C). Deep fry chicken slices until cooked and lift out. Reheat the oil to hot, return the chicken to fry another 10 seconds. Drain and place on a plate.

❸ Keep 1T. oil in the wok, and boil **3** . Pour over chicken, sprinkle on lemon peel and serve.

雞胸肉 300公克	豌豆莢 50公克
1 洋蔥片　50公克 蔥　8段 薑　1片 **2** 醬油、水 　各1大匙 太白粉　2小匙 酒　1小匙	酒　½大匙 **3** 麻油、水 　各1小匙 太白粉　½小匙 味精、胡椒粉、 鹽　各¼小匙

❶ 雞肉洗淨，切成薄片，以 **2** 料醃10分鐘。

❷ 油 2 杯燒至五分熱(120℃)，入雞片過油後撈起，留油 1 大匙爆香 **1** 料，續入豌豆莢、雞片與 **3** 料，拌炒均勻即可。

※ 豌豆肉絲：將雞肉改成豬肉絲，其餘材料及做法均與豌豆雞片同。

※ 豌豆蝦仁：將雞肉改為蝦仁，**2** 料改為蛋白 1 個、太白粉 1 大匙，其餘材料及做法均與豌豆雞片同。

鄉村炸雞
Chicken a la Country

雞半隻 ...... 600公克　　麻油 1大匙

1
- 水、薑末
  - 各1大匙
- 醬油、酒
  - 各½大匙
- 蔥　　　8段
- 胡椒粉、鹽
  - 各¼小匙
- 味精　　⅛小匙

2
- 芹菜末　40公克
- 蔥末　　20公克
- 香菜末　10公克

3
- 辣醬油、檸檬汁
  - 各1大匙
- 花椒粉　¼小匙

❶ 雞洗淨切塊，加**1**料拌勻醃30分鐘。
❷ 鍋熱入油4杯，燒至五分熱(120℃)，放入雞塊以中火炸熟撈起，油再燒熱，雞塊回鍋炸30秒撈起。
❸ 鍋內放入1大匙麻油，入**2**料炒香，再入雞塊拌炒數下，最後再加**3**料拌勻即可。

600g.(1⅓lb.) .... Half chicken
1T. .... Sesame oil

1
- 1T.each Water, minced ginger
- ½T.each Soy sauce, cooking wine
- 8 sections　Green onion
- ¼t.each Salt, pepper

2
- 40g.(1⅖oz.) Minced celery
- 20g.(⅔oz.) Minced green onion
- 10g.(⅖oz.) Minced coriander

3
- 1T.each Worcestershire sauce, lemon juice
- ¼t.Szechwan pepper powder

❶ Wash chicken and cut into serving pieces. Marinate in **1** for 30 minutes.
❷ Heat the wok, add 4C. oil, heat to 248°F (120°C). Fry the chicken pieces until cooked and lift out. Reheat the oil to hot, return chicken to refry for 30 seconds. Remove.
❸ Stir fry **2** with 1T. sesame oil in a wok until fragrant, add in chicken to fry slightly, then add in **3** evenly. Serve.

300g.(10⅔oz.) .... Chicken breast
50g.(1¾oz.) .... Snow pea pod

1
- 50g.(1¾oz.) Sliced onion
- 8 sections　Green onion
- 1 slice　Ginger

2
- 1T.each Soy sauce, water
- 2t.Corn starch
- 1t.Cooking wine

3
- ½T.Cooking wine
- 1t.each Sesame oil, water
- ½t.Corn starch
- ¼t.each Salt, pepper

❶ Wash chicken, cut into thin slices; marinate with **2** for 10 minutes.
❷ Heat the wok, add 2C. oil; heat to 248°F (120°C). Soak chicken slices in hot oil and lift out immediately. Keep 1T. oil in the wok, stir fry **1** until fragrant, add in snow pea pod, chicken and **3**, stir fry and mix well. Serve.
⁕ Shredded pork with snow pea pod: Replace chicken with shredded pork. The rest remains the same as above.
⁕ Shrimp with snow pea pod: Replace chicken with shrimp; **2** with 1 egg white, 1T. corn starch. The rest remains the same as above.

紅油雞丁
Diced Chicken in Chili Oil Sauce

雞腿 450公克
蒜頭花生(圖1) ....
.... 30公克
香菜葉 2大匙

1
蔥　　　　　2段
醬油、麻油
　　　各1大匙
紅油　　½大匙
薑末、鎮江醋、
細糖　各1小匙
鹽　　　¼小匙

❶ 水5杯燒開，入雞腿煮至熟(約15分鐘)，取
出去骨後切丁。蔥亦切成與雞丁相同大小
的小段備用。

❷ 將雞肉丁、花生與**1**料攪拌均勻，以香菜
盤飾即可。

※ 紅油肚條：將雞丁改爲300公克的熟豬肚
條(圖2)，蒜頭花生改爲蔥白，
其餘材料及做法與紅油雞丁同
。

※ 紅油耳絲：將紅油肚條之豬肚改爲250公
克的熟豬耳薄片(圖3)，其餘材
料及做法與紅油肚條同。

450g.(1lb.) .... Chicken leg
30g.(1oz.) .... Garlic peanut (illus. 1)
2T. .... Coriander leaf

1
2 sections Green onion
1T.each Soy sauce, sesame oil
½T.Chili oil
1t.each Minced ginger, black
　　　　vinegar, Sugar
¼t.Salt

❶ Bring 5C. water to boil, boil chicken until cooked (approx. 15 minutes). Remove bone and dice. Dice green onion into same size as chicken.

❷ Mix chicken and peanut with **1** well. Garnish with coriander and serve.

※ Tripe strips in chili oil sauce: Replace chicken with 300g.(10⅗ oz.) cooked pig tripe (illus. 2); peanut with white part of green onion. The rest remains the same as above.

※ Pig ear in chili oil sauce: Replace tripe with 250g.(9oz.) boiled and sliced pig ear (illus. 3). The rest remains the same as tripe recipe above.

小煎子雞
Lightly Fried Chicken Strips

雞腿 .... 600公克　熟筍絲 60公克
芹菜 .... 150公克　辣豆瓣醬 2大匙

1
- 醬油、太白粉、
- 水　　　各1大匙

2
- 紅辣椒片、薑絲
- 　　　各1大匙
- 蔥　　　8段

3
- 醬油、酒
- 　　　各1大匙
- 麻油　　½大匙
- 糖、白醋、水
- 　　　各1小匙
- 太白粉　½小匙
- 味精　　⅛小匙

❶ 芹菜切段，雞腿去骨(圖1)後切成細長條(圖2)，入**1**料醃拌10分鐘備用。

❷ 鍋熱入油4杯燒至六分熱(約140℃)，入雞肉再入芹菜、熟筍絲，隨即一起撈起。

❸ 鍋內留油2大匙炒香辣豆瓣醬，再入**2**料，續入雞條、芹菜、筍絲與**3**料，炒拌均勻即可。

600g.(1⅓lb.) .... Chicken leg
150g.(5⅓oz.) .... Celery
60g.(2¹⁄₁₀oz.) ....
....Boiled and shredded bamboo shoot
2T. .... Hot bean paste

1
- 1T.each Soy sauce, corn starch,
- water

2
- 1T.each Sliced red pepper,
- shredded ginger
- 8 sections Green onion

3
- 1T.each Soy sauce, cooking wine
- ½T.Sesame oil
- 1t.each Sugar, white vinegar,
- water
- ½t.Corn starch

❶ Cut celery into sections. Remove chicken bone (illus. 1) and cut into thin long strips (illus. 2); marinate in **1** for 10 minutes.

❷ Heat the wok, add 4C. oil; heat to 284°F (140°C). Soak chicken first, add celery and bamboo in hot oil. Immediately lift out all togather.

❸ Keep 2T. oil in the wok, stir fry hot bean paste until fragant. Add in **2** , continue with chicken, celery, bamboo, and **3** ; stir fry and mix well. Serve.

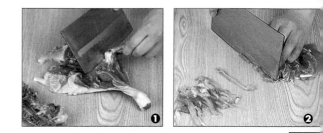

450g.(1lb.) ...Chicken leg (2 pieces)
1T......................... Hot bean paste

1
- ¼t.Szechwan pepper corn
- 2 Dried red pepper

2
- 150g.(5⅓oz.) Diced green pepper
- 30g.(1oz.) Diced red pepper
- 1T.Minced green onion
- 1t.each Minced ginger, minced garlic

3
- 1 Egg white
- ½T.Corn starch
- 1t.Soy sauce

4
- ½T.each Cooking wine, soy sauce
- 1t.each Sugar, sesame oil, water, sugar coloring
- ½t.each White vinegar, corn starch

雞腿2隻 .....450公克　辣豆瓣醬 1大匙

1
- 花椒粒　¼小匙
- 乾辣椒　2條

3
- 蛋白　1個
- 太白粉　½大匙
- 醬油　1小匙

2
- 青椒丁 150公克
- 紅辣椒丁30公克
- 蔥末　1大匙
- 薑末、蒜末　各1小匙

4
- 酒、醬油　各½大匙
- 糖、麻油、水、糖色　各1小匙
- 白醋、太白粉　各¼小匙

❶ 雞腿去骨後切成1.5×1.5公分之小塊，加入❸料醃約15分鐘，乾辣椒切段去籽備用。

❷ 鍋熱入油3杯燒至五分熱(約120℃)，入雞丁過油。撈起後留油3大匙，入❷料炒香後撈起，再入辣豆瓣醬炒香，續入❶料，最後入雞肉、❹料及❷料，炒拌均勻即可。

❶ Bone the chicken legs and cut into 1.5 x1.5 cm small pieces. Marinate in **3** for 15 minutes. Cut dried pepper to sections and discard the seeds.

❷ Heat the wok, add 3C. oil, and heat to 248°F (120°C). Soak chicken in hot oil, lift out immediately and drain. Keep 3T. oil in the wok, stir fry **2** until fragrant; remove. Add in hot bean paste to fry until fragrant, then add in **1** . Finally stir in chicken, **4** , and **2** ; mix evenly and serve.

600g.(1⅓lb.) .... Young chicken
4 pcs .... Lettuce leaf
10g.(⅓oz.) ....Coriander

1
- 3T.Soy sauce paste
- 1T.each Chili oil, sesame oil
- ½T.White vinegar
- 2t.Sesame paste
- 1t.each Garlic paste, Szechwan pepper powder, minced green onion, minced ginger, sugar

嫩雞 600公克
生菜葉..............4片
香菜 10公克

1
- 醬油膏　3大匙
- 辣油、麻油　各1大匙
- 白醋　½大匙
- 芝麻醬　2小匙
- 蒜泥、花椒粉、蔥末、薑末、糖　各1小匙
- 味精　¼小匙

❶ 雞洗淨入開水中煮10分鐘關火，浸泡15分鐘，撈起待涼後，將雞切成 2×5 公分之長方塊，香菜洗淨切段。

❷ 將生菜葉墊盤底，上置雞塊，將❶料拌勻淋在雞塊上，再撒上香菜即可。

❶ Wash chicken and boil in boiling water for 10 minutes. Turn off the fire and soak for another 15 minutes. Drain and cool, cut chicken into 2 x 5 cm rectangular serving pieces. Clean coriander and snip into small sprigs.

❷ Place lettuce leaves on a plate, arrange chicken pieces nicely on top of lettuce. Pour over **1** and sprinkle on coriander. Serve.

怪味雞塊
Chicken with Mixed Flavors

棒棒雞絲
Shredded Bon Bon Chicken

雞半隻 600公克
粉皮 4張
香菜末 10公克
辣油 .... ½大匙

醬油膏　3大匙
芝麻醬　1½大匙
麻油、高湯
　　　　各1大匙
糖、白醋、蔥末
、薑末、蒜末
　　　　各1小匙
花椒粉　½小匙
味精　　¼小匙

600g.(1⅓lb.) ....Half chicken
4 ....Green bean sheet
10g.(⅓oz.) ....Minced coriander
½T. ....Hot pepper oil

3T.Soy sauce
1½T.Sesame paste
1T.each Sesame oil, stock
1t.each Sugar, vinegar, minced
　　　green onion, minced
　　　ginger, minced garlic
½t.Szechwan pepper powder

❶ 雞洗淨，入開水中煮10分鐘關火，浸泡15
分鐘，撈起待涼後，拆成雞絲備用。
❷ 粉皮切粗條，入開水川燙後撈起沖冷水，放
置盤底，上置雞絲，再淋上❶料，撒上香菜
末，最後淋上辣油即可。

❶ Wash chicken, boil in hot water for 10 minutes. Soak for 15 minutes before
remove. When cool, shred chicken with hands.
❷ Cut green bean sheet to long strips; scald in hot water and rinse under cold water.
Place on a platter. Arrange chicken over green bean sheet. Pour ❶ over,
sprinkle coriander, hot pepper oil and serve.

鴨 2400公克
醬油 1大匙

蔥　　　5支
薑　　　6片
鹽、花椒粒
　　　各3大匙
酒、八角
　　　各1大匙

2400g.(5⅓lb.) ....Duck
1T. .... Soy sauce

5　Green onion
6 slices　Ginger
3T.each Salt, Szechwan pepper
　　　corn
1T.each Cooking wine, star
　　　anise

❶ 鴨用❶料全身內外抹勻，醃約30分鐘，再入
鍋蒸60分鐘至熟爛取出，趁熱在鴨身上抹
勻醬油。
❷ 鍋熱入油10杯燒至八分熱(180℃)，將鴨
入鍋大火炸約20分鐘，至金黃色撈起切塊，
排盤即可。

❶ Rub duck with ❶ all over inside out. Marinate about 30 minutes. Steam for 60
minutes to tender. Spread soy sauce over the duck skin while still warm.
❷ Heat the wok, add in 10C. oil; heat to 356°F (180°C). Fry duck over high heat
for about 20 minutes to golden. Lift out and cut into serving pieces. Arrange on a
plate and serve.

香酥鴨
Crispy Duck

鴨............2500公克　　蔥、薑末 各1大匙
糯米..........200公克　　鹽..............1½小匙

1
- 熟豬肚丁、火腿
- 丁、蝦米、香菇
- 丁、筍丁、蓮子
- 、青豆仁、鴨肫
- 丁　　各1大匙

2
- 醬油　　　1大匙
- 酒、麻油
- 　　　各1小匙
- 胡椒粉　　⅓小匙

❶ 將鴨洗淨瀝水，在鴨身內外抹鹽1小匙，醃約60分鐘。

❷ 鍋熱入油2大匙爆香蔥、薑，再入**1**、**2**料炒勻，最後入洗好的糯米及鹽半小匙抖勻即為八寶料。

❸ 將鴨脖子劃一刀(圖1)，去掉整隻鴨骨頭圖2)，然後將八寶料塞入鴨肚內，從鴨脖子處繞一圈打結(圖3)即為八寶鴨。

❹ 將八寶鴨入蒸鍋蒸60分鐘後取出，鍋熱入油10杯燒至八分熱(180℃)，入鴨炸約15分鐘至金黃色即可。

2500g.(5½lb.) ....Duck	
200g.(7oz.) ....Glutinous rice	
1½t. .... Sal	
1T.each...	
.....Minced green onion, minced ginger	

1
- 1T.each Boiled diced pig tripe, diced ham, diced dried hrimp, diced black mushroom, diced bamboo, lotus seed, green pea, diced duck giblet

2
- 1T.Soy sauce
- 1t.each Cooking wine, sesame oil
- ⅓t.Pepper

❶ Wash and dry duck, rub duck inside and outside with 1t. salt, marinate for one hour.

❷ Heat the wok, add 2T. oil; stir fry green onion and ginger until fragant. Add in **1** and **2**, stir fry evenly. Then add in washed glutinous rice and ½t. salt, mix evenly to be the eight treasures filling.

❸ Slit open around the duck neck (illus. 1), take off the whole bone frame (illus. 2). Stuff in the filling, tie a knot around the neck (illus. 3).

❹ Place the duck in a steamer and steam for 60 minutes, remove. Heat the wok, add 10C. oil; heat to 356°F (180°C). Deep fry duck until golden, about 15 minutes. Serve.

樟茶鴨
Camphor and Tea Smoked Duck

............2500公克　　紅辣椒 2條
白 ....6支　　甜麵醬 3大匙
粉（圖1）.. ⅙小匙
　┌ 鹽　　　　3大匙
1│
　└ 花椒粒　　1大匙
　　　　　　　┌ 樟木屑或鋸木屑
　　　　　　　│ （圖2）　　2杯
　　　　　　2│ 陳皮(圖3)、花
　　　　　　　│ 椒粒、八角、茶
　　　　　　　│ 葉　　各1大匙
　　　　　　　└ 白糖　　　1小匙

鍋熱入**1**料炒香，待冷後輾碎與硝粉拌勻備用。

鴨洗淨去細毛，將椒鹽粉用力抹擦在鴨身上，醃置5小時使之入味。

將醃過的鴨抹去椒鹽粉，掛在通風處風乾(約6小時）。

將**2**料置鍋中，上置鐵絲網，鴨子放在網上，蓋上鍋蓋，整鍋移到爐上，用小火燻烤,約10分鐘翻動一次，至鴨身全部呈茶黃色即可。

鴨再入蒸鍋，用大火蒸40分鐘取出。

鍋熱入油8杯燒至八分熱(約180℃)，入鴨大火炸至鴨皮呈金黃色且酥脆，撈出瀝乾，趁熱剁成2×5公分的塊狀，整齊排在盤中。

食時配以蔥白、紅辣椒、甜麵醬即可。

500g.(5½ lb.) ....Duck
.... Green onion (white part only)
T. .... Sweet bean paste
.....................................Red pepper
t. ....Sodium nitrite (illus. 1)
　┌ 3T.Salt
　│ 1T.Szechwan pepper corn
　┌ 2C.Camphor wood chips or other
　│　　wood chips (illus. 2)
　│ 1T.each Dried orange peel (illus.
　│　　3), Szechwan pepper
　│　　corn, star anise, black tea
　│　　leaves
　└ 1t.Sugar

❶ Heat the wok, fry **1** until fragant; when cooled, crash to powder and mix evenly with sodium nitrite.
❷ Wash duck and clean out the fine hair with pincers. Rub pepper salt into duck and marinate for 5 hours.
❸ Wipe off the pepper salt; hang up with a string to dry at a windy place (approx. 6 hours).
❹ Place **2** in a wok, put a metal net over it. Place the duck on the net and cover the wok. Move the wok onto the stove, and smoke over low heat. Turn the duck every 10 minutes. Smoke until the whole duck turns light brown.
❺ Put the duck in a steamer and steam over high heat for 40 minutes.
❻ Heat the wok, add 8C. oil; heat to 356°F (180°C). Deep fry duck until skin golden and crispy. Lift out and drain. While warm, chop to 2 x 5 cm serving pieces. Arange neatly onto a plate.
❼ Serve with green onion, red pepper and sweet bean paste.

❶　　　　　　❷　　　　　　❸

紹子烘蛋
Szechwan Shao-Tze Egg Omelet

蛋	.... 6個	蔥末	...............2大匙
絞肉	.... 50公克	高湯	..................1杯

1
┌ 玉米粉　½大匙
└ 鹽　　　½小匙

3
┌ 鹽　　　1小匙
└ 味精　　¼小匙

2
┌ 筍末　　　60公克
│ 木耳末、榨菜末
└ 　　　各20公克

4
┌ 太白粉、水
└ 　　　各1大匙

❶ 蛋打散,入**1**料打鬆備用。

❷ 鍋熱入油½杯燒至四分熱(100℃),蛋汁
入鍋中,先用大火烘,再改小火烘3分鐘
此時蛋皮兩邊漸漸膨高(圖1),如果中間沒
有膨起,可以另舀一匙油淋在中間(圖2),
蓋上鍋蓋,使蛋全部膨高後,小心用鍋鏟翻
面,待兩面呈金黃色,即可盛起放在圓盤上
,並劃成2公分塊狀(圖3)。

❸ 鍋內餘油先下絞肉炒散,再入**2**料炒香,倒
入高湯煮開加**3**料調味,以**4**料勾芡灑上
蔥末,盛起淋在烘蛋上,即可食用。

6	.... Eggs
50g.(1¾oz.)	.... Minced pork
2T.	..................Minced green onion
1C.	.... Stock

1
┌ ½T.Corn starch
└ ½t.Salt

2
┌ 60g.(2¹⁄₁₀oz.) Minced bamboo
│ 　　　　　shoot
│ 20g.(⅔oz.)each Minced black
│ 　　　　　wood ear, minced
│ 　　　　　pickled heading
└ 　　　　　mustard

3 1t.Salt

4 1T.each Corn starch, water

❶ Beat egg with **1** .

❷ Heat the wok, add ½C. oil; heat to 212°F (100°C). Pour egg into the wok, fry over high heat; then turn to low heat for another 3 minutes. Egg omelet should be puffed up by now (illus. 1); if the center does not puff up, sprinkles spoon oil in the center (illus. 2) and cover with lid. When the omelet puffs up evenly, turn carefully to fry the other side. When golden on both sides, remove to a round plate; and cut into 2 cm pieces (illus. 3).

❸ Reheat the oil in the wok, stir fry minced pork; add in **2** to fry until fragant. Then add in stock and bring to boil, season with **3** ; thicken with **4** . Sprinkle on minced green onion. Pour over egg and serve.

砂鍋豆腐
Bean Curd in Ceramic Pot

腐(嫩)	3塊	粉絲(泡軟後)	70公克
白菜	300公克	中式火腿	30公克
腿	280公克	香菇	5朵
菇	150公克	熟青豆仁	3大匙

1	蔥	4段	**2**	高湯	3杯
	薑	1片		鹽	1小匙
	蝦米	1大匙		味精	½小匙
				胡椒粉	⅓小匙

大白菜洗淨，切成10×2公分之片狀(圖1)，置於砂鍋底(圖2)，上置粉絲(圖3)，另將雞腿煮熟切塊備用。

豆腐切1×5公分薄片，排於粉絲上面。香菇泡軟去蒂切片。

雞腿與火腿片、香菇片、洋菇片鋪於豆腐上，最後灑上青豆仁。

鍋熱入油2大匙爆香**1**料，續入**2**料煮開，淋於砂鍋內，以小火煮約20分鐘即可。

................................Bean curd
0g.(10⅔oz.)........Chinese cabbage
80g.(10oz.)....................Chicken leg
50g.(5⅓oz.) .... Mushroom
0g.(2½oz.) .....Bean thread (softened)
0g.(1oz.)......................Chinese ham
.......................Dried black mushroom
. ... Boiled green pea

1	4 sections Green onion
	1 slice Ginger
	1T.Dried shrimp

2	3C.Stock
	1t.Salt
	⅓t.Pepper

❶ Wash cabbage, cut into 10 x 2 cm serving pieces (illus. 1); place at the bottom of a ceramic cooking pot (illus. 2). Put bean thread over cabbage (illus. 3). Boil chicken until cooked and cut into serving pieces.

❷ Cut bean curd into 1 x 5 cm thin slices; arrange neatly over bean thread. Soften black mushroom with warm water; discard stems and cut to slices.

❸ Spread chicken, ham, black mushroom and mushroom on top of bean curd; at last sprinkle on green peas.

❹ Heat the wok, add 2T. oil; stir fry **1** until fragant. Add in **2** to boil. Pour into ceramic cooking pot and simmer over low heat for 20 minutes. Serve directly from the pot.

麻婆豆腐
Ma-Po's Bean Curd

豆腐 .... 2塊　　辣豆瓣醬 1大匙
絞肉 .... 75公克　　花椒粉 .... ¼小匙
麻油 .... ½小匙　　蔥末 .... 少許

1 ┌ 蔥末　　　 1大匙
　　├ 蒜末、薑末
　　└　　　　 各1小匙

3 ┌ 水　　　　 1大匙
　　└ 太白粉　 1½小匙

2 ┌ 水　　　　 1杯
　　├ 醬油　　 1½大匙
　　├ 酒　　　 1大匙
　　├ 鹽、味精
　　└　　　　 各½小匙

❶ 豆腐切約1公分小塊。
❷ 鍋熱入油2大匙燒熱，入絞肉炒熟(圖1)
　起。餘油加入**1**料爆香，入辣豆瓣醬(圖2
　拌炒，再加**2**料、豆腐與絞肉(圖3)，煮
　即改小火燜煮約3分鐘，以**3**料勾芡成
　汁，灑下蔥末、花椒粉和麻油即可。

2 .... Bean cur
75g.(2⅔oz.) .... Minced por
1T. .... Hot bean pas
½t. .... Sesame c
¼t. .... Szechwan pepper powde
Dash .... Minced green onio

1 ┌ 1T.Minced green onion
　　└ 1t.each Minced garlic, minced
　　　　　　　　 ginger

2 ┌ 1C.Water
　　├ 1½T.Soy sauce
　　├ 1T.Cooking wine
　　└ ½t.Salt

3 ┌ 1T.Water
　　└ 1½t.Corn starch

❶ Cut bean curd into 1 cm cubes.
❷ Heat the wok, add in 2T. oil; stir fry pork until cooked (illus. 1) then remove. Stir fry **1** with remaining oil until fragant. Add in hot bean paste (illus 2) to fry and mix well , then add in **2** ,bean curd and pork (illus. 3). Bring to boil and simmer over low heat for 3 minutes. Thicken with **3** . Sprinkle on minced green onion, Szechwan pepper powder, and sesame oil; serve.

麻辣豆魚
Cold Bean Sprout Rolls with Chili Sauce

綠豆芽 300公克
韭黃. 100公克
豆腐皮 3張

1
醬油　　 2大匙
芝麻醬　 1大匙
糖、麻油、蔥末
　、辣油各½大匙
熟白芝麻 2小匙
白醋　　 1小匙
花椒粉　 ½小匙

1 豆芽菜入水中川燙10秒即全部撈出，用冷
開水沖涼再用手擠乾(圖1)備用。韭黃洗
淨切3公分長段(圖2)。

2 豆腐衣每張切成3小張(圖3)，在每張中包
入豆芽及韭黃，再捲成春捲狀即爲豆魚。

3 鍋熱入油3大匙，入豆魚煎至兩面呈金黃
色，取出切段，食時淋上**1**料即可。

300g.(10⅔oz.) .... Bean sprout
100g.(3½oz.) .... Yellow chive
3 .... Bean curd sheet

1
2T.Soy sauce
1T.Sesame paste
½T.each Sugar, sesame oil, chili
　　　　 oil, minced green onion
2t.Roasted white sesame seed
1t.White vinegar
½t.Szechwan pepper powder

1 Scald bean sprout in boiling water for 10 seconds, lift out and rinse under cold water to cool. Squeeze dry by hand (illus.1). Wash yellow chive and cut into 3 cm sections (illus. 2).

2 Cut each bean curd sheet into 3 small sheets (illus. 3), put bean sprout and chive in the center as filling; roll it into spring roll shapes.

3 Heat the wok, add 3T. oil; fry rolls until golden on both sides. Remove and cut into serving sections. Pour **1** over and serve.

熊掌豆腐
Shrimp Flavored Bean Curd

2 blocks.........................Bean curd		豆腐 2塊		**3**	高湯	1杯
1T. ....Fresh soybean		毛豆 1大匙			醬油	1大匙
¼t. ....Sesame oil		麻油 .... ¼小匙			糖色	½大匙

1 ⎡ 5 slices Chinese ham
⎟ 4 Dried black mushroom
⎣ 1T. Dried shrimp

2 ⎡ 8 sections Green onion
⎣ 4 slices Ginger

3 ⎡ 1C. Stock
⎟ 1T. Soy sauce
⎟ ½T. Sugar coloring
⎟ ½t. Sugar
⎣ ¼t. Pepper

4 1t. each Corn starch, water

1 ⎡ 中式火腿   5片
⎟ 香菇   4朵
⎣ 蝦米   1大匙

2 ⎡ 蔥   8段
⎣ 薑   4片

3 糖 ⅓小匙
味精、胡椒粉
各¼小匙

4 太白粉、水
各1小匙

❶ 豆腐切6×6×1公分方塊，鍋熱入油1杯燒六分熟（140℃），入豆腐半煎半炸至兩面呈金黃色取出。香菇泡軟去蒂切片。

❷ 鍋內留油3大匙，先爆香**2**料，再入**1**料炒香後，入**3**料、豆腐及毛豆，燒煮至汁將收乾時(約3分鐘)，以**4**料勾芡，再淋上麻油即可。

❶ Cut bean curd into 6 x 6 x 1 cm squares. Heat the wok, add 1C. oil and heat to 284°F (140°C). Fry bean curd to golden on both sides and remove. Soften black mushroom in hot water and discard the stems and slice.

❷ Keep 3T. oil in the wok, stir fry **2** until fragant; add in **1** and fry slightly. Then continue with **3** , bean curd and fresh soybean; cook until sauce nearly dried (approx. 3 minutes). Thicken with **4** ; sprinkle on sesame oil, and serve.

豆腐 2塊		**2**	高湯	1⅓杯
絞肉 65公克			醬油	2大匙
蔥末 2大匙			味精	¼小匙
辣豆瓣醬 ... 1½大匙			鹽	⅛小匙
麻油 1小匙		**3**	水	1½大匙

1 ⎡ 薑末、蒜末
⎣   各1小匙

3 太白粉 ½大匙

❶ 每塊豆腐切成1×3×10公分長方塊(圖1)，鍋熱入油6杯燒至七分熟(160℃)，將漏杓先抹油(圖2)，再將豆腐排在漏杓上(圖3)，放入油鍋炸至豆腐浮出油面(約2-3分鐘)，呈金黃色撈起。

❷ 留油2大匙燒熱，入絞肉炒熟，再入豆瓣醬拌炒，隨後入**1**料炒香，再入**2**料及豆腐，改小火燒煮5分鐘，以**3**料勾芡，並加入蔥末、麻油拌勻即可。

家常豆腐
Bean Curd Home Style

紹子豆腐
Szechwan Shao-Tze Bean Curd

豆腐	2塊					2 blocks	Bean curd
絞肉	150公克		水	1杯		150g.(5⅓oz.)	Minced pork
木耳末	3大匙	**2**	醬油	2大匙		3T.	Minced black wood ear
蔥末	1大匙		鹽	½小匙		1T.	Minced green onion
麻油	¼小匙		味精	¼小匙		¼t.	Sesame oil
1 蔥末	1大匙	**3**	太白粉、水				
薑末	1小匙		各1大匙				

1 [1T.Minced green onion
　　 1t.Minced ginger

2 [1C.Water
　　 2T.Soy sauce
　　 ½t.Salt

3 1T.each Corn starch, water

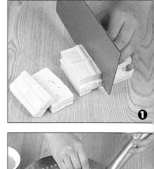

① 豆腐切小塊備用。
② 鍋熱入油¼杯燒熱，入絞肉炒熟續入**1**料炒香，再入木耳、豆腐及**2**料燒煮3分鐘，以**3**料勾芡，並灑上蔥末淋上麻油即可。

① Cut bean curd into small serving cubes.
② Heat the wok, add ¼C. oil, and heat to hot. Stir fry pork until cooked, add in **1** to fry until fragrant. Continue with wood ear, bean curd, and **2** ; cook for 3 minutes and thicken with **3** . Sprinkle on minced green onion and sesame oil. Serve.

2	Bean curd
65g.(2⅓oz.)	Minced pork
2T.	Minced green onion
1½T.	Hot bean paste
t.	Sesame oil

1 [1t.each Minced ginger, minced
　　　　　 garlic

2 [1⅓C.Stock
　　 2T.Soy sauce
　　 ⅛t.Salt

3 [1½T.Water
　　 ½T.Corn starch

① Cut each bean curd into 1 x 3 x 10 cm rectangular pieces (illus. 1). Heat the wok, add in 6C. oil; heat to 320°F (160°C). Grease a sieve (illus. 2) and place bean curd on the sieve (illus. 3). Lower into hot oil and fry until bean curd floats on top of oil (approx. 2 to 3 min.), and golden. Lift out and drain.
② Keep 2T. oil in the wok and reheat to hot, stir fry pork until cooked. Add in hot bean paste to fry, and then add in **1** to fry until fragrant. Continue with **2** and bean curd, turn heat to low and simmer for 5 minutes. Thicken with **3** ; mix in minced onion and sesame oil. Serve.

干貝京白
Cabbage with Dried Scallop

| 600g.(1⅓lb) ....Napa cabbage |
| 37g.(1⅓oz.) ....Dried scallop |

1 ⌈ 2C.Stock
　 ⌊ 1T.Cooking wine
　 　 1t.Salt
2 2T.each　Corn starch, water

大白菜(淨重) ....
　 ....600公克

1 ⌈ 高湯　　　2杯
　 │ 米酒　　　1大匙
　 │ 鹽　　　　1小匙
　 ⌊ 味精　　　¼小匙

干貝 37公克

2 ⌈ 太白粉、水
　　 ⌊ 　　各2大匙

❶ 干貝加1杯水蒸熟，剝成絲備用。
❷ 大白菜入開水中燙軟後撈起，切成對半，莖白再直切三片，加**1**料煮透，撈起白菜置於盤底。
❸ 白菜湯汁與干貝絲及干貝蒸汁煮開，以**2**料勾芡，淋於白菜上即可。

❶ Steam scallop with 1C. water, shred to fine strips by hand. Keep the scallop juice.
❷ Boil cabbage in boiling until tender and drain. Cut to half widthwise, and then cut the white part each into 3 pieces lengthwise. Cook with **1** thoroughly; drain and place on a plate.
❸ Bring cabbage juice, scallop, and scallop juice to boil; thicken with **2**. Pour over cabbage and serve.

| 600g.(1⅓lb.) ....Mustard green |
| 18g.(⅔oz.) ....Dried scallop |
| 2T................................Chicken fat |
| ¼t. ....Baking soda |

1 ⌈ 1C.Stock
　 ⌊ ¼t.Salt
2 2t.each　Corn starch, water

芥菜 600公克
干貝 18公克

1 ⌈ 高湯　　　　1杯
　 │ 鹽、味精
　 ⌊ 　　各¼小匙

雞油 2大匙
鹹塊 ....¼小匙

2 ⌈ 太白粉、水
　　 ⌊ 　　各2小匙

❶ 芥菜洗淨切塊備用。
❷ 10杯水燒開入鹹塊待溶後，入芥菜心煮3分鐘後，取出漂涼水備用。
❸ 干貝加水半杯蒸熟，撕成絲備用。
❹ **1**料及干貝絲、湯入鍋煮開，續入芥菜心燒煮5分鐘，再以**2**料勾芡，灑上雞油即可。

❶ Wash mustard green and cut into serving pieces.
❷ Bring 10C. water to boil, add in baking soda, and boil mustard green for minutes. Drain and rinse under cold water.
❸ Steam scallop in ½C. water. When cooked, shred to thin strips by hand.
❹ Bring **1**, scallop,and scallap juice to boil, add in mustard green, and continu boiling for 5 minutes. Thicken with **2**, sprinkle on chicken fat and serve.

干貝芥菜
Mustard Green with Scallop

冬菇豆苗
Pea Pod Tip with Mushroom

豆苗(淨重) . 300公克
香菇 37公克

1
- 水 2杯
- 豬油、醬油、糖
- 色 各1大匙
- 糖 ½大匙
- 味精 ¼小匙

2
- 水(或高湯) ¼杯
- 酒 1大匙
- 鹽 ⅓小匙
- 味精 ¼小匙

3
- 水 2小匙
- 太白粉、麻油 各1小匙

300g.(10⅔oz.) .... Pea pod tip
37g.(1⅓oz.) Dried black mushroom

1
- 2C.Water
- 1T.each Pork fat, soy sauce, sugar coloring
- ½T.Sugar

2
- ¼C.Stock (or water)
- 1T.Cooking wine
- ⅓t.Salt

3
- 2t.Water
- 1t.each Corn starch, sesame oil

❶ 香菇泡軟去蒂, 每片斜切為二, 油1杯燒至五分熱(120℃), 入香菇炸黃後撈起, 與**1**料燒至湯汁快收乾時, 入**3**料勾芡即可起鍋。

❷ 豆苗去老梗, 洗淨, 鍋熱入油3大匙燒熱, 入豆苗與**2**料炒軟, 隨即起鍋置於盤一邊, 另一邊置香菇即可。

❶ Soften mushroom in warm water and discard the stem. Cut each mushroom into slanting two pieces.   Heat the wok, add 1C. oil and heat to 248°F (120°C). Fry mushroom until cooked, add in **1** ; cook until sauce nearly dried out. Thicken with **3** , and remove.

❷ Wash and discard the tough stem of pea pod tip. Heat the wok, add 3T. oil; add in pea pod tip and **2** , cook until tender.   Remove from the wok and place it on one half side of a platter, and place mushroom on the other half. Serve.

小黃瓜 600公克
蕃茄 3個
雞油 1大匙

1
- 高湯 3杯
- 鹽 1小匙
- 味精 ¼小匙

2
- 高湯 1½杯
- 鹽 ½小匙
- 味精 ¼小匙

3
- 太白粉、水 各1大匙

600g.(1⅓lb.) ....Cucumber
3 ....Tomato
1T................................Chicken fat

1
- 3C.Stock
- 1t.Salt

2
- 1½C.Stock
- ½t.Salt

3 1T.each Corn starch, water

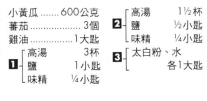

❶ 小黃瓜薄薄削皮, 切成6公分長段, 再切四半去籽, 入開水煮熟取出漂涼備用。

❷ 蕃茄每個切6瓣後, 入水川燙再去皮、籽。

❸ **1**料燒開, 入小黃瓜及蕃茄燒煮3分鐘後, 取出小黃瓜整齊排於盤中, 蕃茄圍於四週, 再將**2**料燒開以**3**料勾芡, 淋於蕃茄黃瓜上, 最後淋上雞油即可。

※ 蕃茄選不要太熟的。

❶ Peel off the skin of cucumber, cut into 6 cm long sections; then cut lengthwise into 4. Boil in boiling water until cooked and rinse under cold water.

❷ Cut tomato into 6 pieces. Scald in boiling water; peel off the skin and discard the seeds.

❸ Bring **1** to boil, add in cucumber and tomato to cook for 3 minutes; remove. Place cucumber neatly on a plate, surrounded by tomato pieces.   Bring **2** to boil and thicken with **3** . Pour over cucumber and tomato; sprinkle on chicken fat and serve.

※ Tomato should not be too ripe.

蕃茄黃瓜
Cucumber with Tomato

450g.(1lb.) .... Eggplant
110g.(3⅘oz.) .... Minced pork
2T. .... Hot bean paste
1T. .... Minced green onion

1 [1T.each Minced garlic, minced ginger]

2 [1C.Stock
1T.each Sugar, soy sauce
1t.Sesame oil]

3 [2t.each Corn starch, water
1t.Vinegar]

茄子 450公克
絞肉 110公克
辣豆瓣醬 2大匙
蔥末 1大匙

1 [蒜末、薑末
各1大匙]

2 [高湯　　　1杯
糖、醬油
　　各1大匙
麻油　　1小匙
味精　　¼小匙]

3 [太白粉、水
　　各2小匙
醋　　1小匙]

❶ 茄子洗淨去皮切10公分長條，6杯油燒至八分熱(180℃)，入茄子炸熟(約6分鐘)撈起備用。

❷ 鍋內留油2大匙，先炒熟絞肉，再入辣豆瓣醬及**1**料炒香，續入**2**料及茄子煮入味後，加**3**料並灑上蔥末即可。

❶ Wash eggplant and peel off the skin, cut into 10 cm long strips. Heat the wok, add in 6C. oil and heat to 356°F (180°C). Fry eggplant until cooked (approx. 6 minutes), drain.

❷ Keep 2T. oil in the wok, stir fry pork, add in hot bean paste and **1**, fry until fragant. Then add in **2** and eggplant; cook until eggplant thoroughly flavored. Thicken with **3** and sprinkle on green onion. Serve.

茄子 225公克
絞肉 250公克
蝦米 2大匙

1 [醬油、麻油
　　各1大匙
太白粉　　½大匙
胡椒粉、味精
　　各¼小匙]

2 [太白粉　2½杯
蛋　　　3個]

3 [辣豆瓣醬　2大匙
薑末、蒜末
　　各1大匙]

4 [高湯　　½杯
糖　　2大匙
酒　　1大匙
太白粉　½大匙
味精　　¼小匙]

5 [蔥末　　4大匙
白醋　　2大匙
麻油　　1大匙]

❶ 茄子洗淨切連刀片(圖1)，蝦米泡軟切末，加入絞肉及**1**料拌成餡備用。

❷ 將餡分別夾入茄夾中即為茄餅(圖2)，**2**料調勻備用。

❸ 鍋熱入油5杯燒至五分熱(120℃)，茄餅沾上**2**料入油鍋(圖3)，以中火炸熟約3分鐘撈起，油再燒熱，茄餅再回鍋炸15秒取出瀝油，置於盤上。

❹ 鍋內留油1大匙爆香**3**料後，續入**4**料煮開，起鍋前加入**5**料淋於茄餅上即可。

雞油菜心
Chicken Flavored Bok Chỏy

青江菜...... 600公克
雞油 .... ½大匙
1 ┌ 高湯   6杯
    └ 鹽   1小匙
2 ┌ 高湯   1杯
    │ 鹽、酒
    │   各½小匙
    └ 味精   ¼小匙
3 ┌ 太白粉、水
    └   各½小匙

600g.(1⅓lb.) .... Bok choy
½T. .... Chicken fat
1 ┌ 6C. Stock
    └ 1t. Salt
2 ┌ 1C. Stock
    └ ½t. each Salt, cooking wine
3 ½t. each Corn starch, water

❶ 青江菜去老葉, 水6杯燒開, 入青江菜川燙
撈起漂涼備用。
❷ **1**料煮開, 入青江菜煮約3分鐘, 撈起置盤
中備用。
❸ **2**料煮開, 入**3**料勾芡, 再加雞油, 淋於青
江菜上即可。

❶ Discard tough leaves on bok choy. Bring 6C. water to boil, parboil bok choy; lift
out to drain and rinse under cold water.
❷ Boil **1** and add in bok choy to cook for 3 minutes. Lift out to place on a plate.
❸ Boil **2** , thicken with **3** , and add chicken fat. Pour over bok choy and serve.

225g.(8oz.) .... Eggplant
250g.(9oz.) .... Minced pork
2T. .... Dried shrimp

1 ┌ 1T. each Soy sauce, sesame oil
    │ ½T. Corn starch
    └ ¼t. Pepper
2 ┌ 2½C. Corn starch
    └ 3 Egg
3 ┌ 2T. Hot bean paste
    └ 1T. each Minced ginger, minced
                garlic
4 ┌ ½C. Stock
    │ 2T. Sugar
    │ 1T. Cooking wine
    └ ½T. Corn starch
5 ┌ 4T. Minced green onion
    │ 2T. White vinegar
    └ 1T. Sesame oil

❶ Wash eggplant and cut into slanting thick pieces with a slit in the center (illus.
1). Soften dried shrimp and mince; mix with pork and **1** to be the filling.
❷ Stuff filling into each slit to be eggplant cake (illus. 2). Mix well to use.
❸ Heat the wok, add in 5C. oil; heat to 248°F (120°C). Dip eggplant cake in **2**
and deep fry (illus. 3) over medium heat until cooked, about 3 minutes; lift out.
Reheat oil to hot, return eggplant cake to fry for 15 seconds. Lift out and drain.
Arrange on a plate.
❹ Keep 1T. oil in the wok, stir fry **3** until fragant; add in **4** to boil. Mix in **5** and
pour over eggplant cake. Serve.

干扁四季豆
Dry Fried String Beans

600g.(1⅓lb.) .... String bean
3T. .... Minced green onion
1t. .... Sesame oil

1
- 150g.(5⅓oz.) Minced pork
- 2T.each Minced dried shrimp, minced pickled heading mustard

2
- ¼C.Water
- 1½T.Soy sauce
- 1T.Sugar

| 四季豆 ...... 600公克 | 麻油 .... 1小匙 |

1
- 絞肉 150公克
- 蝦米末、榨菜末 各2大匙

2
- 水 ¼杯
- 醬油 1½大匙
- 糖 1大匙
- 味精 ¼小匙

❶ 將四季豆去除纖維洗淨，瀝乾水份備用。
❷ 鍋熱入油 3 杯燒至七分熱(160℃)，入四季豆炸成干扁狀撈起備用。
❸ 鍋內留油 1 大匙，放入 **1** 料爆香，再加入四季豆及 **2** 料拌炒均勻，起鍋前加入蔥末及麻油即可。

❶ Wash string bean and discard tough fibers; drain.
❷ Heat the wok, add in 3C. oil, and heat to 320°F (160°C). Deep fry string bean to dry, lift out and drain.
❸ Keep 1T. oil in the wok, stir fry **1** to fragant. Add in string bean and **2** ; mix evenly. Sprinkle on green onion and sesame oil before serving.

春捲皮 12張

1
- 豆芽菜 300公克
- 白豆干絲(圖 1) 100公克
- 紅蘿蔔絲75公克
- 白蘿蔔絲75公克
- 粉絲(泡軟切段) 70公克
- 芹菜段 60公克

2
- 小黃瓜絲 50公克
- 洋火腿絲 40公克
- 洋菜(泡軟切段) 10公克

3
- 麻油 1大匙
- 白醋 ½大匙
- 鹽 1小匙
- 味精 ¼小匙

4
- 芥末醬、冷開水 各½大匙

❶ 將 **1** 料分別入水川燙，取出漂涼後瀝乾，加入 **2** 料及 **3** 料調味，**4** 料調勻於食用前拌入。
❷ 春捲皮分別包入涼菜(圖2及圖3)即可食用。

共和涼菜
Assorted Vegetables in Spring Roll Skin

松子 1杯
生玉米粒 .. 300公克
青椒 75公克
紅辣椒 2條

1
水　　　2大匙
太白粉、麻油
　　　各1大匙
鹽　　　½小匙
味精　　¼小匙

1C. ....Pine nut
300g.(10⅔oz.).....................Corn
75g.(2½oz.) ....Green pepper
2 ....Hot pepper

1
2T. Water
1T. each Corn starch, sesame oil
½t. Salt

❶ 松子洗淨, 鍋熱入油1杯燒至二分熱(60℃),入松子炸至金黃色撈起備用。
❷ 紅辣椒去籽切末, 青椒切丁和玉米粒一起 入油鍋中過油備用。
❸ 鍋中油倒出, 入紅辣椒、玉米粒、青椒及 **1**料炒勻, 起鍋前拌入松子即可。

❶ Wash pine nuts. Heat the wok, add 1C. oil, and heat to 140°F (60°C), fry pine nut until golden.
❷ Discard seeds in pepper and mince. Cut green pepper into cubes. Soak corn, pepper and green pepper in hot oil. Lift out immediately.
❸ Pour off oil. Add pepper, corn, and **1** into the wok ; fry evenly. Mix in pine nut before serving.

---

2 .... Spring roll skin

1
300g.(10⅔oz.) Bean sprout
100g.(3½oz.) Shredded white dried bean curd(illus. 1)
75g.(2⅔oz.) Shredded carrot
75g.(2⅔oz.) Shredded turnip
70g.(2½oz.) Bean thread (softened and sectioned)
60g.(2⅕oz.) Celery sections

2
50g.(1¾oz.) Shredded small cucumber
40g.(1⅖oz.) Shredded ham
10g.(⅓oz.) Agar-agar (softened and sectioned)

3
1T. Sesame oil
½T. White vinegar
1t. Salt

4 ½T. each Mustard, cold water

● Parboil each item in **1** separately, rinse under cold water and dry. Season with **2** and **3** . Mix **4** evenly, and only add in before serving.
● Wrap each spring roll skin with a vegetable filling (illus. 2 and 3). Serve cold.

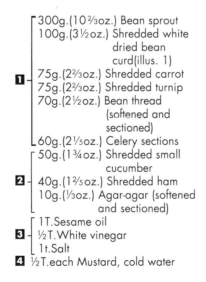

開陽白菜
Dried Baby Shrimp with Napa Cabbage

450g.(1lb.) ....Napa cabbage
18g.(⅗oz.) ....Dried baby shrimp

1 ┌ 1C.Stock
　　└ ½t.Salt
2 ½T.each Corn starch, water

捲心白菜 .. 450公克　　蝦米 18公克
1 ┌ 高湯　　1杯　　**2** ┌ 太白粉、水
　　├ 鹽　　½小匙　　　　└　　　各½大匙
　　└ 味精　　¼小匙

❶ 捲心白菜洗淨切長條, 蝦米先泡軟備用。
❷ 鍋熱入油2大匙爆香蝦米, 入白菜炒軟, 再
　入**1**料拌勻燜煮片刻, 以**2**料勾芡即可。

❶ Wash cabbage and cut into serving long strips. Soften shrimp with warm water.
❷ Heat the wok, add 2T. oil; stir fry shrimp until fragant. Add in cabbage, cook until tender. Then mix in **1** evenly and braise for a while. Thicken with **2** and serve.

冬瓜(淨重)1000公克　　蛋白 3個
中式火腿末..75公克　　雞油 2大匙
干貝 ....20公克　　蔥末 1大匙
1 ┌ 雞湯　　3杯　　**2** ┌ 水　　2大匙
　　├ 鹽　　¾小匙　　　　└ 太白粉　1大匙
　　├ 胡椒粉、味精
　　└　　　各¼小匙

❶ 冬瓜去皮、籽切塊(圖1), 入蒸籠蒸20分
　鐘取出, 入果汁機內打成泥備用。
❷ 蛋白打發, 干貝加水½杯蒸熱(圖2), 撕成
　絲(圖3)備用。
❸ 鍋熱入油2大匙, 續入冬瓜泥及干貝並加
　1料煮開, 以**2**料勾芡, 灑上蔥末, 鍋熄火
　入蛋白拌勻盛盤。
❹ 雞油燒熱淋在蛋白上, 最後灑上火腿末即
　可。

冬瓜雪
Snowy Winter Melon

高麗菜 300公克	冷開水 6杯	
蘿蔔 300公克	白醋 6大匙	
辣椒 30公克	糖 6大匙	
薑片 20公克	鹽 1½大匙	

● 高麗菜洗淨，完全擦乾水份撕成小塊。白
蘿蔔洗淨去皮、切成薄片。辣椒去籽洗淨
切段。

● 將所有材料放置一乾淨、有蓋的容器中，
泡置二天二夜即可食用。

300g.(10⅔oz.) .. Chinese cabbage	
300g.(10⅔oz.) .... Turnip	
30g.(1oz.) .... Hot pepper	
20g.(⅔oz.) .... Sliced ginger	
6C. .... Cold water	
6T.each .... White vinegar, sugar	
1½T. .... Salt	

● Wash cabbage, dry thoroughly; tear to small pieces. Wash and skin turnip; cut into thin slices. Discard the seeds and cut pepper into sections.

● Place all the materials in a clean container with lid; soak for two full days, then ready to eat.

1000g.(2⅕lb.)	
.... Winter melon (net weight)	
75g.(2⅔oz.)...Minced Chinese ham	
20g.(⅔oz.)................Dried scallop	
......................................Egg white	
T. ....Chicken fat	
T. .... Minced green onion	

1 ⎰ 3C.Chicken stock
⎱ ¾t.Salt
⎱ ¼t.Pepper

2 ⎰ 2T.Water
⎱ 1T.Corn starch

Skin winter melon and discard the seeds (illus. 1). Put into a steamer and steam for 20 minutes. Puree it in a juicer.

Beat egg white to stiff. Steam scallop with ½C. water until cooked (illus. 2); shred by hand to fine shreds (illus. 3).

Heat the wok, add in 2T. oil; pour in melon puree, scallop and **1** ; bring to boil and thick with **2** . Sprinkle on minced green onion. Turn off the heat, mix in egg white evenly and place onto a deep plate.

Heat chicken fat to hot, pour over egg white; sprinkle on minced ham and serve.

一品豆腐湯
Supreme Bean Curd Soup

嫩豆腐 180公克
雞柳肉 45公克
竹笙 30公克

1
蛋白　　　 2個
鹽　　　 1/3小匙
味精、胡椒粉
　　　　各1/4小匙

2
蔥葉、髮菜、中
式火腿、冬瓜皮
、紅蘿蔔各少許

3
高湯　　 4杯
鹽　　 1/2小匙
味精　 1/3小匙

❶ 將豆腐攪爛成泥；雞胸肉用刀背搥成雞泥備用。

❷ 竹笙用水泡軟洗淨，切5公分長段，入熱水川燙備用。

❸ 豆腐泥、雞茸及**1**料攪拌均勻後，取一盤盤底抹油(圖1)後舖上豆腐泥並抹平(圖2)，再以**2**料裝飾(圖3)所要之圖案，隨入蒸籠蒸7分鐘。

❹ **3**料入鍋煮開後，加入竹笙煮熟，倒於湯碗中，再將豆腐滑入湯中即可。

180g.(6 1/3oz.)......................Bean curd
30g.(1oz.)...
.... Dried bamboo pith (chu Sheng)
45g.(1 2/3oz.)..........Chicken breast fillet

1
2 Egg white
1/3t.Salt
1/4t.Pepper

2
Dash each Green onion, black
　　　　moss, chinese ham,
　　　　winter melone peel,
　　　　carrot

3
4C.Stock
1/2t.Salt

❶ Beat bean curd to mash; with back of a knife beat chicken to mash.

❷ Soften dried bamboo pith with water and wash clean; cut into 5 cm long sections. Scald in boiling water and drain.

❸ Mix bean curd mash, chicken mash and **1** together evenly. Grease the bottom of a plate (illus. 1), spread on mash mixture and scrape surface smooth (illus. 2); decorate with **2** (illus. 3). Steam for seven minutes.

❹ Bring **3** to boil, add in bamboo; boil until cooked. Pour into a large soup bowl; slide in steamed bean curd and serve.

酸辣湯
Hot and Sour Soup

高湯	5杯		醬油	2大匙
蛋	2個	**2** 鹽	3/4小匙
麻油	1/2大匙		味精	1/3小匙

豆腐	270公克		烏醋、白醋
鴨血	100公克		各1½大匙
海參	100公克	**3** 蔥末、薑末
豬肉	50公克		各2小匙
發泡魷魚	50公克		胡椒粉 1小匙
濕木耳	40公克	**4** 水 2大匙
			太白粉 1大匙

❶ 湯碗中放入 **3** 料, 蛋打勻備用。

❷ **1** 料切絲入高湯中同煮, 待煮開後加入 **2** 料, 再以 **4** 料勾芡, 隨即倒入蛋液, 再倒入 湯碗中, 並淋上麻油即可。

※ 可依個人的口味, 增減胡椒粉與醋。

5C.	Stock
2	Egg
½T.	Sesame oil

270g.(9½oz.)	Bean curd
100g.(3½oz.)	Duck blood
100g.(3½oz.)	Sea cucumber
50g.(1¾oz.)	Pork
50g.(1¾oz.)	Cuttlefish (soaked)
40g.(1²/₅oz.)	Black wood ear

◀ 2T.Soy sauce
3/4t.Salt

◀ 1½T.each Brown vinegar, white
vinegar
2t.each Minced green onion,
minced ginger
1t.Pepper

◀ 2T.Water
1T.Corn starch

❶ Put **3** into a large soup bowl. Beat the eggs.

❷ Shred all meterials in **1** and boil with stock. After boiling, add in **2** and thicken with **4** . Pour in egg, then pour back to soup bowl. Sprinkle on sesame oil and serve.

※ Volume of vinegar and pepper depends on personal taste.

清燉牛肉湯
Clear Beef Soup

300g.(10⅔oz.) ....Beef brisket	牛腩 300公克
5C...Stock	高湯 5杯

1
- 1　Green onion
- 3 slices　Ginger
- 1T.Cooking wine
- ½T.Salt
- ½t.Szechwan pepper corn

1
- 蔥　　　　1支
- 薑　　　　3片
- 酒　　　1大匙
- 鹽　　　½大匙
- 花椒粒　½小匙

❶ 牛腩川燙後切成 3 公分方塊。
❷ 高湯煮開入 **1** 料及牛腩再入鍋蒸 3 小時即可。

❶ Parboil beef and cut into 3 cm cubes.
❷ Bring stock to boil, add in **1** and beef. Steam for 3 hours and serve.

全瘦絞肉 ...120公克	
菠菜 75公克	
芹菜末 1大匙	

1
- 粉絲(泡軟後切段)　70公克
- 濕木耳片40公克
- 榨菜片　20公克

2
- 蛋白　　　½個
- 水　　　　1大匙
- 太白粉　　1小匙
- 蔥末、薑末　各½小匙
- 胡椒粉、鹽　各¼小匙

3
- 高湯　　　5杯
- 鹽　　　　1小匙
- 味精　　　½小匙
- 胡椒粉　　¼小匙

❶ 絞肉入 **2** 料, 順同一方向用力攪勻成肉漿(圖1), 菠菜洗淨切 3 公分長段, 均備用。
❷ **3** 料煮開後改小火, 將肉漿擠成12個小肉丸, 入鍋煮至浮起(圖2), 再入 **1** 料及菠菜煮熟, 起鍋前灑上芹菜末即可。

川丸子湯
Meat Ball Soup

榨菜肉絲湯
Shredded Pork Soup with Pickled Mustard

白菜 .... 70公克　　雞油 1小匙

里肌肉絲
　　　 120公克
竹筍絲　60公克　　**2** ┌ 高湯　　6杯
榨菜絲　50公克　　　　├ 鹽　　　1小匙
冬粉(泡軟切段)　　　　└ 胡椒粉　⅛小匙
　　　 70公克

里肌肉加⅓杯水拌匀, 小白菜洗淨切段備用。

2料燒開, 加入**1**料煮2分鐘。

小白菜置湯碗中, 趁熱將湯沖入碗中, 最後淋上雞油即可。

70g.(2½oz.) .... Young cabbage
1t. .... Chicken fat

1 ┌ 120g.(4⅕oz.)Shredded pork
　　│　　　　loin
　　│ 60g.(2oz.)Shredded bamboo
　　│　　　　shoot
　　│ 50g.(1⅘oz.)Shredded pickled
　　│　　　　heading mustard
　　└ 70g.(2½oz.)Bean thread
　　　　(softened and sectioned)

2 ┌ 6C.Stock
　　├ 1t.Salt
　　└ ⅛t.Pepper

Mix pork with ⅓C. water. Wash cabbage and cut into serving pieces.
Bring **2** to boil, add in **1** to cook 2 minutes.
Place cabbage in a large soup bowl, pour hot soup over; sprinkle on chicken fat
and serve.

20g.(4⅕oz.) . Grounded lean pork
5g.(2⅔oz.)..................... Spinach
T. .... Minced celery

1 ┌ 70g.(2½oz.) Bean thread
　　│　　(softened and sectioned)
　　│ 40g.(1⅖oz.) Sliced black
　　│　　　wood ear
　　└ 20g.(⅔oz) Sliced pickled
　　　　heading mustard

2 ┌ ½ Egg white
　　│ 1T.Water
　　│ 1t.Corn starch
　　│ ½t.each Minced green onion,
　　│　　　minced ginger
　　└ ¼t.each Salt, pepper

3 ┌ 5C.Stock
　　├ 1t.Salt
　　└ ¼t.Pepper

Mix pork with **2** ; beat clockwise until becoming meat paste (illus. 1). Wash
spinach and cut into 3 cm long sections.
Bring **3** to boil and turn heat to low. Squeeze meat paste into 12 small meat
balls. Cook meat balls in soup until floating (illus. 2). Then add in **1** and
spinach; cook until spinach is cooked. Sprinkle on celery and serve.

600g.(1⅓lb.)	Winter melon	冬瓜	600公克		水	4杯
300g.(10⅔oz.)	Chicken leg	雞腿	300公克		蔥	1支
37g.(1⅓oz.)	Chinese ham	中式火腿	37公克	**1** 薑	1片
15g.(½oz.)	Dried black mushroom	干貝	20公克		酒	1大匙
20g.(⅔oz.)	Dried scallop	冬菇	15公克		鹽	1小匙

1
- 4C.Water
- 1 Green onion
- 1 slice Ginger
- 1T.Cooking wine
- 1t.Salt

❶ 冬瓜去皮去籽切2公分立方，雞腿切3公分方塊，入鍋川燙並洗淨，中式火腿切片，干貝加水1杯蒸軟(約20分鐘)取出拆絲，冬菇泡軟去蒂切片。

❷ 先將冬瓜放入燉盅中，依序擺上雞腿、冬菇、火腿、干貝，再入**1**料蒸90分鐘即可。

❶ Pare winter melon and remove the seeds; cut into 4 cm cubes. Cut chicken into cm cubes; parboil and rinse clean. Slice ham. Steam scallop with 1C. water un soften (approx. 20 minutes) and shred by hands. Soften mushroom with war water; remove stem and slice.

❷ Place winter melon in a ceramic pot, put in sequence of chicken, mushroom, han scallop and **1** over melon. Steam 90 minutes and serve.

90g.(3⅕oz.)	Pork kidney	豬腰	90公克	熟豬肚	80公	
80g.(2⅘oz.)	Precooked pork maw	里肌肉	75公克	小黃瓜	60公	
75g.(2⅔oz.)	Pork fillet	粉絲	40公克	榨菜	20公	
60g.(2¹⁄₁₀oz.)	Small cucumber	雞油	1小匙			
40g.(1⅖oz.)	Bean thread					
20g.(⅔oz.)	Pickled heading mustard	**1** 醬油、太白粉		**2** 高湯	5	
1t.	Chicken fat	各1小匙		鹽	¾小	

1 1t.each Soy sauce, corn starch

2
- 5C.Stock
- ¾t.Salt

❶ 里肌肉切薄片，入**1**料醃約10分鐘，榨菜片，小黃瓜切成長片狀，粉絲用水泡軟備。

❷ 豬肚先加水煮至熟爛後切片。

❸ 里肌肉入開水川燙，豬腰去除白筋洗淨片川燙，兩者均鋪於湯碗中備用。

❹ **2**料燒開，隨即放入榨菜、肚片、小黃、粉絲煮2分鐘，倒入湯碗中再加雞油可。

❶ Cut pork fillet into thin slices and marinate with **1** . Cut cucumber into obl slices. Soften bean thread with warm water.

❷ Cook pork maw until very tender and slice.

❸ Parboil pork in boiling water. Trim off white sinew of kidney, cut into slices; parboil, place both at the bottom of a large soup bowl.

❹ Bring **2** to boil, add in pickled mustard, pork maw, cucumber, and bean thre cook for 2 minutes. Pour into the soup bowl, sprinkle on chicken fat, and serve.

黃瓜三片湯
Cucumber Gourmet Soup

冬菇鮑魚湯
Abalone with Black Mushroom Soup

灌頭鮑魚 ...100公克	筍片 60公克	100g.(3½oz.) ....Canned abalone	
豆苗 20公克	香菇 3朵	60g.(2 1/10 oz.) .. Sliced bamboo shoot	
高湯 5杯	雞油 1大匙	20g.(⅔oz.) .... Pea pod tip	
1 ┌ 鹽 1小匙		5C. ....Stock	
└ 味精 ¼小匙		3 .... Dried black mushroom	
		1T. ....Chicken fat	
		1t. .... Salt	

❶ 香菇泡軟去蒂切片, 鮑魚切片, 豆苗洗淨備用。

❷ 高湯煮開放入香菇、筍片、鮑魚煮2分鐘, 入**1**料調味。

❸ 豆苗置湯碗中, 趁熱將湯沖入碗中, 最後淋上雞油即可。

❶ Soften black mushroom with hot water, discard the stems, and slice. Cut abalone into thin slices and wash pea pod tip.

❷ Bring stock to boil, add in mushroom, bamboo, and abalone; cook for 2 minutes and season with salt.

❸ Place pea pod tip in a large soup bowl; pour hot soup over, and sprinkle on chicken fat. Serve.

白蘿蔔 300公克	┌ 高湯 6杯	300g.(10⅔oz.) .... Turnip	
五花肉 150公克	**1** ├ 花椒粒 1小匙	150g.(5⅓oz.) .... Pork bacon	
薑 5片	└ 鹽 ½小匙	5 slices .... Ginger	
蔥 4段		4 sections .... Green onion	
雞油 1小匙		1t. ....Chicken fat	
		1 ┌ 6C.Stock	
		├ 1t.Szechwan pepper corn	
		└ ½t.Salt	

❶ 豬肉洗淨入鍋煮熟, 待涼切大薄片, 蘿蔔去皮直切成8×3公分薄片, 備用。

❷ **1**料燒開, 隨入蘿蔔片以小火煮25分鐘, 再入豬肉片及蔥、薑, 起鍋前將蔥、薑挑掉, 倒入湯碗中, 淋上雞油即可。

❶ Wash pork and boil until cooked. When cool, cut into large thin slices. Pare turnip and cut into 8 x 3 cm thin slices.

❷ Bring **1** to boil, add in turnip, and turn down heat to simmer for 25 minutes. Then add in pork, green onion and ginger. Discard green onion and ginger before serving. Pour into a soup bowl, sprinkle on chicken fat, and serve.

連鍋湯
Turnip Soup

三絲魚翅羹
Shark's Fin Potage with Shredded Chicken

發好魚翅 ...110公克			**2** 蔥	2支
筍絲 120公克			薑	3片
雞胸 100公克			醬油、酒 各2大匙	
香菇 15公克			糖	1小匙
雞油 2大匙			胡椒粉	⅓小匙
1 蔥	2支		**3** 水	2大匙
薑	2片		太白粉	1大匙
酒	2大匙			

❶ **1**料加水燒開後,入魚翅川燙撈起洗淨,香菇泡軟去蒂切絲,雞胸肉切絲,加太白粉1小匙及水1大匙拌勻備用。

❷ 油3杯燒熱,雞絲入油鍋中過油。

❸ 鍋入高湯5杯,再入魚翅、筍絲、香菇、雞肉及**2**料,燒開後改小火煮約30分鐘後再以**3**料勾芡淋上雞油即可。

110g.(3⁴⁄₅oz.) . Shark's fin (pre soaked)
120g.(4⅕oz.) Shredded bamboo shoot
100g.(3½oz.) .... Chicken breast
15g.(½oz.) ....Dried black mushroom
2T. .... Chicken fat

1	2	Green onion
	2 slices	Ginger
	2T.	Cooking wine
2	2	Green onion
	3 slices	Ginger
	2T.each	Soy sauce, cooking wine
	1t.	Sugar
	⅓t.	Pepper
3	2T.	Water
	1T.	Corn starch

❶ Scald shark's fin in boiling water with **1** ; drain and wash clean. Soften mushroom with warm water, discard stems and shred. Shred chicken breast, marinate with 1t. corn starch and 1T. water.

❷ Heat the wok, add 3C. oil ; heat to hot. Soak chicken in hot oil; lift out immediately.

❸ Add 5C. stock, shark's fin, bamboo, mushroom, chicken and **2** ,bring to boil and simmer over low heat for 30 mimutes. Thicken with **3** ;sprinkle on chicken fat then serve.

紅燒牛肉麵
Noodle in Beef Soup

麵條	600公克
牛肉	300公克
小白菜	2棵
蔥	10段
薑	3片
辣豆瓣醬	2大匙
花椒粒	1小匙

1
醬油	7大匙
糖色、酒	各1大匙
糖	1小匙
味精	1/3小匙
鹽	1/4小匙

❶ 牛肉用開水川燙洗淨，切成3公分小塊備用。

❷ 鍋熱入油3大匙，將辣豆瓣醬炒香，再下花椒粒稍炒，隨即入水10杯、蔥、薑、**1**料及牛肉，煮開後，改小火燜煮至牛肉熟爛備用(約1小時40分鐘)。

❸ 小白菜入開水中燙熟。

❹ 麵條入沸水煮熟，撈起瀝水置於湯碗中，淋上牛肉湯，再加上牛肉及小白菜即可。

600g.(1⅓lb.)	Noodle
300g.(10⅔oz.)	Beef brisket
2	Baby cabbage
10 sections	Green onion
3 slices	Ginger
2T.	Hot bean paste
1t.	Szechwan pepper corn

1
- 7T. Soy sauce
- 1T. each Sugar coloring, cooking wine
- 1t. Sugar
- ¼t. Salt

❶ Parboil beef, rinse clean. Cut into 3 cm cubes.

❷ Heat the wok, add 3T. oil; stir fry hot bean paste until fragant. Add in pepper corn to fry slightly. Then add in 10C. water, green onion, ginger, **1** ,and beef. Bring it to boil, and simmer over low heat until beef is tender (approx. 1 hour 40 minutes).

❸ Boil cabbage in boiling water until cooked.

❹ Boil noodle until cooked, lift out and drain; place in a soup bowl. Pour beef soup in, place beef and cabbage on top; serve.

酸辣麵
Spicy and Sour Mein

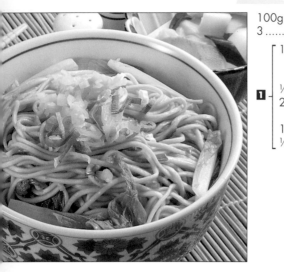

100g.(3½oz.) .... Noodle (Mein)
3 .... Young cabbage

| **1** | 1T.each Chili oil, brown vinegar, minced green onion
½T.Soy sauce
2t.Minced pickled heading mustard
1t.Garlic paste
½t.Szechwan pepper powder |

麵條 100公克
小白菜 3棵

| **1** | 辣油、鎮江醋、蔥花　各1大匙
醬油　½大匙
榨菜末　2小匙
蒜泥　1小匙
花椒粉　½小匙
味精　¼小匙 |

❶ 將 **1** 料混合均勻即爲酸辣汁, 備用。
❷ 麵條入開水中煮熟, 再入白菜煮開, 撈起瀝乾, 與酸辣汁拌勻即可。

❶ Mix all materials in **1** evenly to be spicy and sour sauce.
❷ Boil noodle in boiling water until cooked, add in cabbage; bring to boil again, drain and mix with sauce. Serve.

雞胸肉 300公克
麵條 600公克
綠豆芽 150公克
小黃瓜 2條
麻油 3大匙
鹽 1小匙

| **1** | 蔥末　3大匙
薑泥、蒜泥　各1大匙 |

| **2** | 涼高湯　⅔杯
醬油　5大匙
芝麻醬、麻油　各3大匙
紅油、細糖、白醋　各1½大匙
花椒粉　¾小匙
鹽　½小匙
味精　⅓小匙 |

❶ 麵條入開水煮熟後撈出, 沖冷水後瀝乾(避免黏成一團), 以 3 大匙麻油拌開, 吹涼備用。
❷ 雞胸肉入開水煮 5 分鐘, 取出待涼拆絲。綠豆芽燙過開水後, 以冷開水漂涼備用。小黃瓜刨絲, 加鹽醃10分鐘後, 洗去鹽份。**1**、**2** 料調勻爲調味汁備用。
❸ 將綠豆芽置盤底, 依序放上麵條、小黃瓜絲與雞絲, 最上面再淋上調味汁, 食時拌勻即可。

雞絲涼麵
Spiced Cold Chicken Noodles

擔擔麵
Dan Dan Mein

麵條......... 100公克
小白菜 3棵
花生粉 1小匙

1
高湯　　1½大匙
蔥花、芝麻醬
　　　　各1大匙
醬油　　½大匙
榨菜末、鎮江醋
、麻油　各2小匙
蒜泥　　1小匙
糖、花椒粉
　　　　各½小匙

100g.(3½oz.) .... Noodle (Mein)
3 .... Young cabbage
1t............................ Peanut powder

1
1½T.Stock
1T.each Minced green onion,
　　　　sesame paste
½T.Soy sauce
2t.each Minced pickle heading
　　　　mustard,brown vinegar,
　　　　sesame oil
1t.Garlic paste
½t.each Sugar, Szechwan
　　　　pepper powder

❶ **1**料在碗中調勻成糊狀, 小白菜洗淨切3
公分長段。
❷ 麵條入開水中煮熟, 再入小白菜煮開後一
同撈起瀝乾, 放置碗中, 淋上**1**料, 再撒上
花生粉即可。

❶ Mix **1** in a bowl evenly to paste. Wash cabbage and cut into 3 cm long strips.
❷ Boil noodle in boiling water until cooked, then add in cabbage to reboil. Lift out and drain; place in a bowl. Pour over **1**, sprinkle on peanut powder and serve.

300g.(10⅔oz.) .... Chicken breast
600g.(1⅓lb.) .... Noodle
150g.(5⅓oz.) .... Bean sprout
2............................ Small cucumber
3T. .... Sesame oil
1t..Salt

1
3T. Minced green onion
1T.each Minced ginger, minced
　　　　garlic

2
⅔C.Stock (cold)
5T.Soy sauce
3T.each Sesame paste, sesame
　　　　oil
1½T.each Chili oil, sugar, white
　　　　vinegar
¾t.Szechwan pepper powder
½t.Salt

❶ Boil noodle until cooked; drain and rinse under cold water, drain and dry thoroughly (otherwise noodle will stick together). Mix in 3T. sesame oil, spread out to cool.
❷ Add chicken into boiling water to cook for 5 minutes; shred to fine shreds when cool. Parboil bean sprout in boiling water; rinse under cold water to cool and drain. Shave cucumber to fine threads, marinate with salt for 10 minutes; wash off salt and pat dry. Mix **1** and **2** together evenly to be noodle sauce.
❸ Place bean sprout at the bottom of a large plate, next put on noodle, cucumber and chicken. Pour on the sauce and serve. Mix well before eating.

紅油抄手
Spicy Baby Wontons

餛飩皮 .... 20張　　絞肉 80公克

1
- 水　　　　　　1小匙
- 太白粉、麻油
  　　　　各¼小匙
- 胡椒粉、鹽
  　　　　各⅓小匙

2
- 辣油、蒜泥
  　　　　各2大匙
- 醬油　　1⅓大匙
- 糖、蔥末
  　　　　各2小匙
- 醋　　　1小匙
- 味精、花椒粉
  　　　　各¼小匙

❶ 將絞肉與**1**料拌勻爲肉餡。將每一張餛飩皮包入1小匙肉餡(圖1)，先對折成三角型，再折成半(圖2)，最後兩角對疊(圖3)成型。

❷ 水2杯煮開，放入餛飩，待煮開浮起後撈出放置碗內，將**2**料拌勻淋在餛飩上即可。

20 .... Wonton skin (small)
80g.(2⁴/₅oz.) .... Minced pork

1
- 1t. Water
- ¼t. each Corn starch, sesame oil
- ⅛t. each Salt, pepper

2
- 2T. each Chili oil, garlic paste
- 1⅓T. Soy sauce
- 2t. each Sugar, minced green onion
- 1t. vinegar
- ¼t. Szechwan pepper powder

❶ Mix well pork and **1** to be wonton filling. Place a filling at the center of a wonton skin (illus. 1), fold corner to corner to form a triangle; then fold into half again (illus. 2), finally pinch togather two corners (illus. 3).

❷ Bring 2C. water to boil, add in wonton. When water boils and all wontons float on top, lift out wontons and place in a bowl. Mix well **2** and sprinkle over wonton; serve.

味全家政班

味全家政班創立於民國五十年，經過三十餘年的努力，它不只是國內歷史最悠久的家政研習班，更成為一所正式學制之外的專門學校。

創立之初，味全家政班以教授中國菜及研習烹飪技術為主，因教學成果良好，備受各界讚譽，乃於民國五十二年，增闢插花、工藝、美容等各門專科，精湛的師資，教學內容的充實，深獲海內外的肯定與好評。

三十餘年來，先後來班參與研習的學員已近二十萬人次，學員的足跡遍及台灣以外，更有許多國外的團體或個人專程抵台，到味全家政班求教，在習得中國菜烹調的精髓後，或返回居住地經營餐飲業，或擔任家政教師，或獲聘為中國餐廳主廚者大有人在，成就倍受激賞。

近年來，味全家政班亟力研究開發改良中國菜餚，並深入國際間，採集各種精緻、道地美食，除了樹立中華文化「食的精神」外，並將各國烹飪口味去蕪存菁，擷取地方特色。為了確保這些研究工作更加落實，我們特將這些集合海內外餐飲界與研發單位的經典之作，以縝密的拍攝技巧與專業編輯，出版各式食譜，以做傳承。

薪傳與發揚中國烹飪的藝術，是味全家政班一貫的理念，日後，也將秉持宗旨，永續不輟。

Wei-Chuan Cooking School

Since its establishment in 1961, Wei-Chuan Cooking School has made a continuous commitment toward improving and modernizing the culinary art of cooking and special skills training. As a result, it is the oldest and most successful school of its kind in Taiwan.

In the beginning, Wei-Chuan Cooking School was primarily teaching and researching Chinese cooking techniques. However, due to popular demand, the curriculum was expanded to cover courese in flower arrangements, handcrafts, beauty care, dress making and many other specialized fields by 1963.

The fact that almost 200,000 students, from Taiwan and other countries all over the world, have matriculated in this school can be directly attributed to the high quality of the teaching staff and the excellent curriculum provided to the studends. Many of the graduates have become successful restaurant owners and chefs, and in numerous cases, respected teachers.

While Wei-Chuan Cooking School has always been committed to developing and improving Chinese cuisine, we have recently extended our efforts toward gathering information and researching recipes from defferent provinces of China. With the same dedication to accuracy and perfection as always, we have begun to publish these authentic regional gourmet recipes for our devoted readers. These new publications will continue to reflect the fine tradition of quality our public has grown to appreciate and expect.

More Wei-Chuan Cook Books

純青出版社

劃撥帳號：12106299
地址：台北市松江路125號4樓
電話：(02) 2508-4331、2506-3564
傳真：(02) 2507-4902

Distributor: Wei-Chuan Publishing

1455 Monterey Pass Rd., #110
Monterey Park, CA 91754, U.S.A.

Tel: (323) 2613880・2613878

Fax: (323) 2613299

家常菜
- 226道菜
- 200頁
- 中文版

營養便當
- 147道菜
- 96頁
- 中文版

家常100
- 100道菜
- 96頁
- 中英對照

Favorite Chinese Dishes
- 100 recipes
- 96 pages
- Chinese/English Bilingual

素食
- 84道菜
- 120頁
- 中英對照

Vegetarian Cooking
- 84 recipes
- 120 pages
- Chinese/English Bilingual

健康素
- 76道菜
- 96頁
- 中英對照

Simply Vegetarian
- 76 recipes
- 96 pages
- Chinese/English Bilingual

微波食譜第一冊
- 62道菜
- 112頁
- 中英對照

Microwave Cooking Chinese Style
- 62 recipes
- 112 pages
- Chinese/English Bilingual

微波食譜第二冊
- 76道菜
- 128頁
- 中英對照

Microwave Cooking Chinese Style 2
- 76 recipes
- 128 pages
- Chinese/English Bilingual

養生家常菜
- 80道菜
- 96頁
- 中英對照

Chinese Home Cooking for Health
- 80 recipes
- 96 pages
- Chinese/English Bilingual

實用烘焙
- 77道點心
- 96頁
- 中英對照

International Baking Delight
- 77 recipes
- 96 pages
- Chinese/English Bilingual

飲茶食譜
- 88道菜
- 128頁
- 中英對照

Chinese Dim Sum
- 88 recipes
- 128 pages
- Chinese/English Bilingual

養生藥膳
- 73道菜
- 128頁
- 中英對照

Chinese Herb Cooking for Health
- 73 recipes
- 128 pages
- Chinese/English Bilingual

廣東菜
- 75道菜
- 96頁
- 中英對照

Chinese Cuisine Cantonese Style
- 75 recipes
- 96 pages
- Chinese/English Bilingual

嬰幼兒食譜

- 140道菜
- 104頁
- 中文版

無油煙食譜

- 46道菜
- 68頁/菊16開
- 中文版

快手菜食譜

- 49道菜
- 68頁/菊16開
- 中文版

美容餐食譜

- 50道菜
- 68頁/菊16開
- 中文版

下午茶食譜

- 40道菜
- 68頁/菊16開
- 中文版

米食-家常篇

- 84道菜
- 96頁
- 中英對照

米食-傳統篇

- 82道菜
- 96頁
- 中英對照

麵食-家常篇

- 91道菜
- 96頁
- 中英對照

麵食-精華篇

- 87道菜
- 96頁
- 中英對照

美味小菜

- 92道菜
- 96頁
- 中英對照

Rice
Home Cooking

- 84 recipes
- 96 pages
- Chinese/English Bilingual

Rice
Traditional Cooking

- 82 recipes
- 96 pages
- Chinese/English Bilingual

Noodles
Home Cooking

- 91 recipes
- 96 pages
- Chinese/English Bilingual

Noodles
Classical Cooking

- 87 recipes
- 96 pages
- Chinese/English Bilingual

Appetizers

- 92 recipes
- 96 pages
- Chinese/English Bilingual

健康食譜

- 100道菜
- 120頁
- 中英對照

上海菜

- 91道菜
- 96頁
- 中英對照

台灣菜

- 73道菜
- 120頁
- 中英對照

庖廚偏方　庖廚錦囊　庖廚樂

- 中文版

Healthful Cooking

- 100 recipes
- 120 pages
- Chinese/English Bilingual

Chinese Cuisine
Shanghai Style

- 91 recipes
- 96 pages
- Chinese/English Bilingual

Chinese Cuisine
Taiwanese Style

- 73 recipes
- 120 pages
- Chinese/English Bilingual

純青食譜 養生系列　您健康的好伙伴

健康素
Simply Vegetarian

養生藥膳　四季皆宜

寓藥於食的《養生藥膳》，每道菜皆由中醫師陳旺全臨床對症應用，是匯集了保五臟、四季皆宜及產後的養生佳餚。

本書作法詳實，材料易得，讓吃與健康相得益彰。

養顏七珍雞（作法詳見養生藥膳第89頁）
七樣珍貴中藥材，爽口補身四季宜，氣血雙補功效好！

養生藥膳
Chinese Herb Cooking for Health

健康素　告別油膩

不忌蔥蒜，標榜低油、低鹽的《健康素食譜》，教您快手輕鬆做；素材豐富，口感多變，拉開素食的新視野，讓您吃得更健康。

彭家豆腐（作法詳見健康素食譜第49頁）
彭家豆腐易上手，二大步驟即上菜，煎一煎、灑下料，美味就在嘴裡面。

養生家常菜　健康動起來

《養生家常菜》以健康養生為訴求，教您如何依身體需求烹調營養美食，本書並增列生機篇，讓您自己在家培育生機蔬菜，再以最簡單原始的技巧享受美味。

食療兼備，讓健康事半功倍。

紅棗鱸魚湯（作法詳見養生家常菜第84頁）
鮮美紅棗鱸魚湯，味道清淡好料理，去風寒、調體質，全家健康總動員。

養生家常菜
Chinese Home Cooking for Health

健康食譜
Healthful Cooking

健康食譜　吃出健康

《健康食譜》強調「平衡飲食」、「天然食品」、「清淡食品」之價值與補療重要性。

本書除適用一般減肥者參考外，更針對糖尿病、腎臟病等慢性病患者，提供可輔助醫療效果之食譜，讓您藉此享受健康飲食。

肉捲芹菜　（作法詳見健康食譜第11頁）
牛肉芹菜鴛鴦配、健康美味齊報到，燙一燙、煎一煎，全家愛吃都稱好。